Popular Culture and High Culture

POPULAR CULTURE AND HIGH CULTURE

An Analysis and Evaluation of Taste

HERBERT J. GANS

BasicBooks
A Division of HarperCollinsPublishers

For David Riesman

Library of Congress Cataloging in Publication Data

Gans, Herbert J.
    Popular culture and high culture; an analysis and
evaluation of taste.

    Includes bibliographical references.
    1.   United States—Popular culture.   2.   United
States—Intellectual life.   I.   Title
E169.12.G36   1975   301.2'1   74-79287
Cloth: ISBN: 0-465-06021-8
Paper: ISBN: 0-465-09717-0

20 19 18 17 16

Contents

Preface   vii

INTRODUCTION
*Mass Culture, Popular Culture,
and Taste Culture*   1

The Future of the Mass Culture Critique   4
Some Definitions   9

CHAPTER ONE
The Critique of Mass Culture   17

Popular Culture's Defects as a Commercial Enterprise   20
Popular Culture's Danger to High Culture   27
Popular Culture's Impact on Its Audience   30
Popular Culture's Harmfulness to Society   43
The Sources and Biases of the Mass Culture Critique   51

CHAPTER TWO
*A Comparative Analysis of High
and Popular Culture*   65

Taste Cultures and Publics   69

The Five Taste Publics and Cultures   75
"Youth," Black, and Ethnic Cultures   94
The Social Structure of Taste Publics and Cultures   103

CHAPTER THREE

The Evaluation of Taste Cultures and Publics

                                                          119

Two Value Judgments about Taste Cultures and Publics   125
Cultural Mobility   129
Cultural Pluralism and Subcultural Programming   132
The Pros and Cons of Subcultural Programming   136
Implementing Subcultural Programming   146
The Outlook for More Cultural Pluralism   156

Notes   161
Index   173

Preface

THIS BOOK is a sociological study of popular culture and high culture, and of their place in American society. It is also a critical study, defending popular culture against some of its attackers, particularly those claiming that only high culture is a culture, and that popular culture is a dangerous mass phenomenon. I believe both to be cultures and my analysis therefore looks at both with the same conceptual apparatus. The apparatus itself is sociological, but it rests on two value judgments: (1) that popular culture reflects and expresses the aesthetic and other wants of many people (thus making it culture and not just commercial menace); and (2) that all people have a right to the culture they prefer, regardless of whether it is high or popular. In its conclusions, the book is thus an argument for cultural democracy and an argument against the idea that only the cultural expert knows what is good for people and for society. Finally, the book is a study in cultural policy, for it ends by translating its values and findings into some policy proposals for more cultural pluralism.

Popular culture is not studied much these days either by social scientists or humanists, except in the pages of the new *Journal of Popular Culture*, although the 1970s have seen a revival of social-science research interest in the mass media, particularly the news and entertainment fare of television. I suppose one reason for the lack of interest in popular culture is the anticommercial bias with which many scholars look at culture; they often deem it worthy of attention only if it is created by unpaid folk and by "serious" artists who do not appear to think about earning a living.

In an era in which America is racked by economic, political, and racial crises, the lack of scholarly interest in popular culture may also be due to the relative lack of importance of the topic. How people create and use popular culture is properly of lower priority these days than how people deal with society's crises. Still, even though popular culture does not often concern itself with or comment on these crises, it does so at times, and it ought to be looked at at least from this perspective: to see what it has to say about the various crises, how people use and respond to what it tells them, whether this feeds back into public opinion and political decision making, and if so how, when, and when not.

This is only a currently topical and specific version of a more general question that ought to be asked: How important is popular culture in society? Is it merely a commercially concocted activity for the leisure hours, which goes in one eye or ear and out the other, or does it reflect both shallow and deep-lying, manifest and latent, assumptions, values, wishes, and even needs in American society? Are the ever-changing fashions in television programs and characters only novelties invented by producers looking for a different way to entertain the audience and to score high Nielson ratings? Or are these fashions what George Gerbner calls cultural indicators of changes in the lives and attitudes of Americans, and of the uses which audiences make of popular culture and the gratifications they receive from it?

This leads to a second and related question: Is popular culture something that is created in New York and Hollywood by skilled profit-seeking enterprises which have enough of a monopoly over the supply of entertainment and information that they can impose almost anything they think will sell on the American public, particularly on the television public—a captive audience to a handful of channels? Or are these enterprises themselves often unwitting agents of a culture in the anthropological sense, of a shared set of values or norms that they must try to express if they arc to attract an audience and make their profits?

I do not have final answers to either question. I am inclined to think that popular culture, or at least that part of it transmitted by the mass media, tends to go in one eye and out the other, and that most individual television programs, movies, and magazines are ephemeral for most people. On the other hand, the mass media are ever-present and they offer descriptions of and commentary on many aspects of American life, so that they may be expressing or reflecting what at least some members of the media audience are thinking and dreaming about. And believing this, I cannot subscribe to the notion that popular culture is simply imposed on the audience from above, but I believe that it is shaped by that audience, at least in part, albeit indirectly. The mass media, and perhaps all of commercial popular culture, are often engaged in a guessing game, trying to figure out what people want, or rather, what they will accept, although the game is made easier by the fact that the audience must choose from a limited set of alternatives and that its interest is often low enough to make it willing to settle for the lesser of two or three evils. Still, the media executives who become successful by guessing correctly can often sense what an audience will accept, and frequently they are so firmly embedded themselves in the popular culture to which they are adding that they are "representatives" of the audience, even if they may also be tough-minded and cynical businessmen and women at the same time.

A Summary of
the Argument

The book addresses itself indirectly to both questions, but concerns itself primarily with an analysis of the relationship—and conflict—between high culture and popular culture. It begins, in Chapter One, with an examination of the so-called mass culture critique, which has argued for a long time that popular culture is an aberration born of commercial greed and public ignorance. After analyzing the many specific charges laid against popular culture, I conclude that almost all are groundless and that popular culture does not harm either high culture, the people who prefer it, or the society as a whole.

The argument in Chapter One is in part comparative, showing that the differences between high culture and popular culture have been exaggerated; and the similarities, underestimated. The comparative analysis is expanded in Chapter Two, which proposes that popular culture is, like high culture, a taste culture, chosen by people who lack the economic and educational opportunities of the devotees of high culture. Moreover, I suggest that America is actually made up of a number of taste cultures, each with its own art, literature, music, and so forth, which differ mainly in that they express different aesthetic standards. This is an unoriginal idea that has been around for a long time in the popular distinction between highbrow, middlebrow, and lowbrow—except that my analysis does not view the latter two as any better or worse than the first. Moreover, this trilogy is too simple. Therefore the chapter identifies and describes five taste cultures, subdivides them further into conservative, progressive, and other factions, and then examines also the youth, black, and other racial and ethnic cultures that came into being or into visibility during the 1960s.

The underlying assumption of this analysis is that all taste cultures are of equal worth; this assumption is translated into an evaluative principle in Chapter Three. Because taste cultures reflect the class and particularly educational attributes of their publics, low culture is as valid for poorly educated Americans as high culture is for well-educated ones, even if the higher cultures are, in the abstract, better or more comprehensive than the lower cultures. This principle suggests two policy alternatives: (1) "cultural mobility," which would provide every American with the economic and educational prerequisites for choosing high culture; and (2) "subcultural programming," which encourages all taste cultures, high or low. I opt for subcultural programming and suggest some ways by which all taste cultures could grow, particularly those of publics which are now poorly served by the mass media.

My findings, judgments, and policy proposals obviously differ sharply from those of conservative, socialist, and radical critics of popular culture, but they are also unlikely to please the conservative intellectuals who like, or at least tolerate, popular culture because it is not radical or because it is marketed via free enterprise. Finally, while the book is not often critical of mass media fare, it does not defend the media as institutions. The media are mainly interested in paying customers, but I think everyone should get the culture they want, even if they cannot afford to pay for it.

Acknowledgments

My primary debt is to David Riesman, my teacher, colleague, and, above all, friend, to whom this book is dedicated. Some twenty-five years ago, he encouraged me to develop further a scholarly interest in popular culture and the mass media which had begun with my writing about them for my high school newspaper. He not only assured me that popular culture was a proper topic for a sociologist—and an aspiring graduate student—in an era when it was not considered legitimate by most sociologists, but he also listened respectfully to my ideas and shared his ideas with me. Indeed, he set up an exchange of ideas in which teacher and student were equals, which did wonders for my morale and helped generate the self-confidence that is so necessary for exploring ideas and doing research. The many discussions I had with him—and with Nathan Glazer and Reuel Denney when all three were working on *The Lonely Crowd*—have left their mark on my study, although I must add that they bear no responsibility for it and may not agree with its conclusions.

The book is a much revised and expanded version of my essay "Popular Culture in America," which appeared in Howard S. Becker, ed., *Social Problems: A Modern Approach* (New York: Wiley, 1966). I am grateful to John Wiley and Sons for allowing me to publish the book; to Bill Gum who encouraged and edited the initial essay when he was at Wiley, and who encouraged me to write the book when he was at Basic Books; and to Stimson Bullitt and the Bullitt Foundation for a grant which helped me to write the initial essay. Alice Liftin and Audrey McGhie typed the manuscript of the book faultlessly and quickly. Finally, I am grateful to my wife Louise for her critical reading of the manuscript. She corrected some of its faults; I am wholly responsible for those that remain.

INTRODUCTION

Mass Culture, Popular Culture, and Taste Culture

IN heterogeneous societies, the struggles between diverse groups and aggregates over the allocation of resources and power are not limited to strictly economic and political issues, but also extend to cultural ones. In America, as in all Western societies, the longest and perhaps most important cultural struggle has pitted the educated practitioners of high culture against most of the rest of society, rich and poor, which prefers the mass or popular culture provided by the mass media and the consumer goods industries. Intellectually, that struggle has actually been a one-sided debate. The advocates of high culture criticize popular culture as a mass culture which has harmful effects on both individuals consuming it and on society as a whole, while the users of popular culture ignore the critique, reject high culture, and continue to patronize the sellers of media fare and consumer goods.

The so-called mass culture critique is important because it is concerned with far more than media fare and consumer goods. It is really about the nature of the good life, and thus about the purpose of life in general, particularly outside the work role. It is also about which culture and whose culture should dominate in society, and represent it as the societal or national culture in the competition between contemporary societies and in the historical record of cultures or civilizations. As such, the mass culture critique is an attack by one element in society against another: by the cultured against the uncultured, the educated against the uneducated, the sophisticated against the unsophisticated, the more affluent against the less affluent, and the cultural experts against the laity. In each case, the former criticize the latter for not living up to their own standard of the good life.

The Future of the Mass Culture Critique

The mass culture critique is endemic to urban-industrial society, and has existed ever since daily life became divided into periods of work and free time, particularly among the poor. In modern society, as Leo Lowenthal and Marjorie Fiske have shown, the critique originated in the eighteenth century with the beginnings of popular literature, a forerunner of today's mass media, and while even today it continues to emphasize symbolic culture, in print or on a screen, it also expanded to other spheres of life.[1] Since the nineteenth century, the critique has worried about leisure behavior in general, at least in America: at first about the popularity of alcohol and illicit sex, and later about the passivity of spectator sports and film or television viewing, the fear being that with increasing leisure time, the more intensified use of mass culture would lead to boredom, discontent, and possibly even social chaos. With respect to leisure facilities, in the nineteenth century and the early twentieth century, the critique emphasized the allegedly harmful effects of the music hall, the tavern, and the brothel; from about the 1920s to the 1950s, it focused on the movies, comic books, radio, and spectator sports. During the affluence of the 1950s, it expanded its concern to mass consumption in general, and to the suburban life-style in particular, but in the 1960s it narrowed again, centering now mainly on the negative effects of television viewing. The changing emphases of the critique did not represent a change in the critique itself, however; rather, the critics chose to attack whatever then seemed most popular, or at least most visible or threatening to them in the off-work behavior of most Americans.

Since the late 1960s, however, the critique has undergone two substantial changes in direction. On the one hand, some of the critics dropped their attack on popular culture because they identified a new and greater enemy, the so-called youth culture, which they criticized for its political radicalism, hedonism, mysticism, and nihilism. The change of target was in part a response to the attack of youth culture spokesmen on high culture, for radicals such as Herbert Marcuse argued that high culture was sometimes as much the servant of an oppressive and antirevolutionary ruling class as mass culture, and Marcuse's argument was repeated with considerably less politeness by his younger colleagues. In a sense, the erstwhile critics of mass culture accepted the validity of Marcuse's charge, for at least some now began to see positive features in mass culture's conservatism, perhaps with the hope, probably unconscious, that the defenders of mass culture would join with them to fight against the new, and as they saw it, common enemy.

The other change of direction has been even more drastic, suggesting at least by implication an end to the mass culture critique because high culture ideas had been accepted by and in popular culture. Thus, Nathan Glazer has written that:

Until the fifties, the distinction highbrow, middlebrow, and lowbrow was critical in discussing American culture. They have now quite disappeared . . . because highbrow ideas . . . have by now captured the old audience of the middlebrow.[2]

Daniel Bell went even further, arguing that the old class conflict between high and mass culture had disappeared

5

because, for a significant part of the population, cultural choices were no longer determined by class position:

Art [by which he means high culture art] has become increasingly autonomous, making the artist a powerful taste-maker in his own right; the "social location" of the individual (his social class or other position) no longer determines his life-style and his values. ... For the majority of the society ... this general proposition may still hold true. But it is increasingly evident that for a significant proportion of the population, the relation of social position to cultural style, particularly if one thinks in gross dimensions such as working class, middle class and upper class—no longer holds.[3]

Glazer and Bell are quite correct to suggest that high culture standards and ideas have diffused more widely throughout the society, and have become more acceptable as well, at least in the upper-middle class. Even so, the distinction between high culture and popular culture has not disappeared; even a cursory look at an evening television program schedule or a magazine rack indicates that popular culture is still very different from high culture. Moreover, the youth culture of the 1960s has now declined, at least in public visibility, and no longer looks as threatening to the advocates of high culture as it did only a few years ago. Indeed, much of that youth culture is now being incorporated into commercial popular culture. The Rolling Stones may have replaced the Beatles and Elvis Presley in the pantheon of popular singers, but while their music and the cultural and political themes of their lyrics differ from those of their predecessors, they appeal to the same audience of young people and are handled by the same record companies. Thus, as the youth culture of the 1960s becomes part of the dominant popular culture of the 1970s, the differences between popular and high culture may once again widen, thus providing at least the raw material for a revival of the mass culture critique.

There is, however, a more important reason to suspect a revival of the critique. Actually, the existence of the critique has less to do with changes in high and popular culture than with the position of intellectuals in society, particularly those intellectuals who are or feel themselves to be part of the "Establishment"; over time, the critique has appeared when intellectuals have lost power and the status that goes with power, and it has virtually disappeared when intellectuals have gained power and status. Thus, the critique reached its apogee during the late 1940s and 1950s, not so much because of the rising affluence of that period and the dramatic expansion of consumer goods and other popular culture products which accompanied it, but because the affluence, status, and power of intellectuals during that period did not rise as well, and actually declined as a result of the "cultural apathy" of the Eisenhower era and Senator Joseph McCarthy's savage attacks on left-wing and liberal intellectuals. Conversely, the critique declined during the 1960s not only because of the flowering of youth culture, but also because intellectuals rose considerably in income, power, and status during the Kennedy and Johnson eras.

Two current trends in American society suggest, however, that another decline of intellectual status may be in the offing, and I suspect that the critique will soon return to a high position on the intellectual agenda. The first trend is the current academic depression, which struck the universities—where most practitioners of high culture are now to be found—during the Vietnam war, and which is now continuing partly because of the shrinkage of the university-age population cohort, and partly because of the federal government's economic and political policies. Not only are students, who are after all, the potential recruits for the next generation's high culture, losing their fellowships, but the Nixon Administration consciously tried to downgrade the influence of liberal and left-wing intellectuals—and other profes-

7

sionals—in American life even as it increased public subsidies for the arts. And if these Nixon administration policies continue under President Ford, and more important, to have popular support in Middle America, intellectual criticism of Middle America's popular culture is likely to be resuscitated.

A second source of potential threat to the position of intellectuals comes from a very different political trend—the current revival of egalitarian ideas in America. Its impetus stems largely from nonintellectual sources: from students, women, blacks and other unequally treated populations, and from a rising dissatisfaction with economic inequality among Middle Americans whose expectations for a higher standard of living have been frustrated by the combined recession-inflation which began in the late 1960s.[4] Although some intellectuals are taking part in this revival, others, particularly humanist intellectuals, are opposing it, for they see more equality as a source of danger to high culture. Their view is by no means entirely irrational, for insofar as the economic vitality of high culture depends on very rich people who are its customers and patrons, and who subsidize the magazines, museums, concerts, and other institutions which disseminate high culture, more economic equality might reduce their numbers, or at least reduce the amount of money they have to spend on and in behalf of high culture.[5] In addition, some defenders of high culture fear that greater equality would threaten the meritocratic basis on which high culture is said to be selected, and that other bases, including the recruitment of women and racial and ethnic minorities to institutions of high culture, would dilute the quality of high culture and the standards by which it is judged.[6]

Although both fears are understandable, I believe they will turn out to be groundless, for whatever changes the current demands for equality bring about in America, the users of high culture have sufficient prestige and power to protect their interests. For example, even if income redistribution reduced the spending power of the very rich, governmental and foundation subsidies for high culture would take up the slack; and even if the current meritocracy of *credentialism* were altered so that additional able women and racial and ethnic minority group members were hired by high culture institutions, the meritocracy of *performance* would not need to be violated, and the same combination of critical and audience judgment that now determines the standards and content of high culture would prevail. Nevertheless, the fears of high culture advocates are not likely to be stilled, and these fears may encourage some of them to be critical of egalitarian demands, and of the Middle Americans who make them. Thus, it is possible that the mass culture critique will be revived for use as an argument against the egalitarian trend.

Whatever the future ups and downs of the mass culture critique, however, this book is less concerned with the conflict between high and popular culture than with understanding them both. It is also concerned with the more fundamental question of what roles both high and popular culture play in American society, partly to arrive at policies which would replace cultural conflict with cultural coexistence—or pluralism—and would encourage greater creativity in all cultures, high and popular.

Some Definitions

Before proceeding to these topics, I want to define some of the basic concepts which will appear in this book, particularly mass culture, popular culture, and *taste culture*, a term that encompasses them both. The term *mass culture* is a combination of two German ideas: *Masse* and *Kultur.* The mass is (or was) the nonaristocratic, uneducated portion of European society, especially the people who today might be described as lower-middle class, working class, and poor.

9

Kultur translates as *high culture*; it refers not only to the art, music, literature, and other symbolic products that were (and are) preferred by the well-educated elite of that European society but also to the styles of thought and feelings of those who choose these products—those who are "cultured." Mass culture, on the other hand, refers to the symbolic products used by the "uncultured" majority.

The term *mass culture* is obviously pejorative; *mass* suggests an undifferentiated collectivity, even a mob, rather than individuals or members of a group; and *mass culture*, that mob's lack of culture. This negative judgment can be counteracted by the use of more positive terms like *popular culture* or *popular arts*, and I shall use them instead. But even these terms assume the existence of two kinds of culture, high and popular, which are so different that they cannot be compared, thus positing an initial dichotomy which then shapes all subsequent analysis. For example, Dwight MacDonald rejects the term popular culture because a work of high culture is sometimes also popular and justifies the term mass culture because "its distinctive mark is that it is solely and directly an article for mass consumption."[7] Consequently, he argues that, by definition, high and popular culture cannot be compared.

In reality, however, there are a number of popular cultures, and they as well as high culture are all *taste cultures* which function to entertain, inform, and beautify life, among other things, and which express values and standards of taste and aesthetics. When these taste cultures are compared, high culture turns out to be similar in many ways to the others.

Taste cultures, as I define them, consist of values, the cultural forms which express these values: music, art, design, literature, drama, comedy, poetry, criticism, news, and the media in which these are expressed—books, magazines, newspapers, records, films and television programs, paintings and sculpture, architecture, and, insofar as ordinary consumer goods also express aesthetic values or functions, furnishings, clothes, appliances, and automobiles as well. In addition, taste cultures include the values, forms, and media of the natural and social sciences and philosophy—including their commercial popularizations and even "folk wisdom." Finally, taste cultures have political values; although they do not often express them explicitly, they do so implicitly, and even when not, they frequently have political implications.

The concept of taste culture is an abstraction; it separates the values people express and practice from the people themselves. This is justifiable only for analytic purposes, for culture does not exist apart from people who create and use it, except perhaps in unvisited museums. Consequently, it is necessary to distinguish between taste culture, the *creators* of that culture, and its *users*. Users who make similar choices of values and taste culture content will be described as publics of an individual taste culture, or *taste publics*, even though they are unorganized aggregates rather than organized publics.

Taste culture includes the media that transmit cultural content and the mass media which also supply it. At times, I use popular culture and media fare interchangeably because so much of today's popular culture is media fare. Still, some popular culture continues to be created in the home and community by cultural amateurs—and more so than the tenor of my analysis will suggest.

Furthermore, I do not assume an absolute correlation between people's aesthetic values and the output of the media, and whether the media in fact express the values of their taste publics is an empirical question which still remains to be answered. Indeed, judging by the dissatisfaction with media fare occasionally reported in opinion polls, there is reason to doubt that they always do so. Furthermore, cultural values cannot be inferred from cultural content, at least not without knowing how people choose content, and it

11

may be that when they choose something from the mass media—or from high culture, for that matter—they do not do so because it expresses their values, but only because they like it better than something else, or because it is the lesser of two evils. Similarly, taste publics are defined primarily in terms of shared aesthetic values, rather than because they choose the same cultural content, for they may choose it on the basis of different values. Until more is known about the relationship between available cultural products and people's aesthetic values, and between their choices from the available products and their values, it is, however, sometimes necessary to assume, as I will do in the chapters to follow, that the existing cultural fare expresses people's values and that taste publics making the same cultural choices do so on the basis of similar values.

Taste culture has been defined broadly here; its boundaries are very large, but they are narrower than the boundaries of the concept of culture used by anthropologists. The boundaries of taste culture can be demarcated in several ways. One way is to restrict taste culture to the culture of leisure or free time, but this is too narrow, because leisure values cannot be separated from non-leisure values. Another demarcation would limit taste culture to the aesthetic, but this forces an overly rigid distinction between aesthetic and utilitarian values. I would demarcate taste culture as the culture which results from choice; it has to do with those values and products about which people have some choice. For example, refrigerators are today an accepted product of the larger American culture and it is difficult to live without them. Which of the various kinds and styles of refrigerators to buy is a matter of relatively free choice—except for people who lack the money or the space to choose from the most expensive models—and that choice involves an application of taste culture.

Conversely, political attitudes and activities cannot properly be classified as taste culture, although taste does play a role, for in many respects, one's politics is not a matter of choice. Insofar as people's political values are determined by economic position, occupation, or religion, choice is restricted, and choice is restricted further by the lack of "products" which express people's values. Thus, while some factory workers are Republicans, their political values differ from those of corporation executives who vote for the same party, but neither can find a party which expresses only their own values. They must choose from what is offered them, and sometimes they too can select only the lesser of two evils even if they would prefer something else. Taste plays a political role mainly in the choice of electoral candidates; since politicians run for office as persons and not just as professional politicians, they inevitably communicate their own cultural status. Adlai Stevenson was often described as an "egghead" because he appeared to be most comfortable with high culture, and with voters who preferred high culture, but most national politicians fall—and want to be perceived to fall—within the middlebrow range.

In addition, taste culture is a *partial* culture, for it provides values and products for only a part of life, and except for a handful of high and popular culture addicts, and some of the professionals who create culture, it is not a *total* way of life.[8] Even though taste culture is partial, it is tied to the rest of culture, because the values of taste culture are often similar to other values people hold, for example, about work or family life. Indeed, one reason for the existence of many taste cultures is the fact that America is culturally pluralist, made up of a number of subcultures which coexist around a common core—"American culture"—even though that core is so vague and so limited both in content and adherents that no one has ever succeeded in delineating it satisfactorily. Consequently, the taste cultures are probably more correctly described as subcultures.

Finally, taste culture is, for most people most of the time, a *vicarious* culture; it is not the *lived* culture which can be abstracted from the way people actually live, but a culture which describes how the fictional characters of entertainment fare and the real characters of the news stories act. The relationship between the vicarious culture and the lived culture, or between art and life, is very complex; sometimes one imitates another, but most often they travel along separate paths, with a variety of impacts on each other. Some people, the aforementioned addicts and professionals, live their taste culture, but most people treat it as something outside themselves, to be used for information, enjoyment, self-realization, therapy and escape. Despite a great deal of research, the effects of the vicarious culture on the lived culture, and the functions which the former has for people have not yet been determined adequately.[9]

A brief list of other terms which will come up in the book may also be helpful. *Popular culture* will sometimes be used to describe all the taste cultures except high culture. *Taste cultures* are composed of content or products or cultural items; and by *content* I may mean a film or only themes within a film. By *creators of cultural content* I mean both the so-called serious artist of high culture and the popular artist, writer, or director employed in the mass media—but I shall also distinguish between *creators* and *decision makers*. (For example, a film producer who supervises the making of a film is a decision maker rather than a creator—although in television, the producer also plays a creative role, for he is actually the equivalent of a film director.) I use the term *aesthetic* broadly, referring not only to standards of beauty and taste but also to a variety of other emotional and intellectual values which people express or satisfy when they choose content from a culture, and I assume, of course, that people apply aesthetic standards in all taste cultures, and not just in high culture.[10] Some of these terms are borrowed from marketing, and although they may lack stylistic appeal, they facilitate the comparative analysis. The assumption that taste cultures can be compared is obviously central to my argument, and provides the basis for both the analysis and evaluation to follow.

CHAPTER ONE

The Critique of Mass Culture

THE critique of mass or popular culture is now about two hundred years old, and in its contemporary form, that critique emphasizes four major themes:

1. *The negative character of popular culture creation.* Popular culture is undesirable because, unlike high culture, it is mass-produced by profit-minded entrepreneurs solely for the gratification of a paying audience.
2. *The negative effects on high culture.* Popular culture borrows from high culture, thus debasing it, and also lures away many potential creators of high culture, thus depleting its reservoir of talent.
3. *The negative effects on the popular culture audience.* The consumption of popular culture content at best produces spurious gratifications, and at worst is emotionally harmful to the audience.
4. *The negative effects on the society.* The wide distribution of popular culture not only reduces the level of cultural quality—or civilization—of the society, but also encourages totalitarianism by creating a passive audience peculiarly responsive to the techniques of mass persuasion used by demagogues bent on dictatorship.

Each of these charges will be discussed in some detail, although I cannot describe all the separate arguments that go into the charges or indicate differences of opinion among individual critics.[1] Then I will present evidence for and against these charges. Unfortunately, little empirical research is available to test the factual statements in these charges, and

19

I will sometimes rely on personal observations, impressions, and even speculation.[2] Many of the charges rest on value premises which cannot be studied empirically, and in this case I shall analyze the assumptions implicit in them, questioning those that seem unwarranted or undesirable to me.[3]

Popular Culture's Defects
as a Commercial Enterprise

The criticism of the process by which popular culture is created consists of three related charges: that mass culture is an industry organized for profit; that in order for this industry to be profitable, it must create a homogeneous and standardized product that appeals to a mass audience; and that this requires a process in which the industry transforms the creator into a worker on a mass production assembly line, requiring him or her to give up the individual expression of his own skill and values.

For example, Lowenthal writes:

The decline of the individual in the mechanized working processes of modern civilization brings about the emergence of mass culture, which replaces folk or "high" art. A product of popular culture has none of the features of genuine art, but in all its media popular culture proves to have its own genuine characteristics: standardization, stereotypy, conservatism, mendacity, manipulated consumer goods.[4]

Dwight MacDonald puts it more sharply:

Mass Culture is imposed from above. It is fabricated by technicians hired by businessmen; its audience are passive consumers, their participation limited to the choice between buying and not buying. The Lords of *Kitsch*, in short, exploit the cultural need of the masses in order to make a profit and/or to maintain their class rule.[5]

Implicit in these charges is a comparison with high culture, which is portrayed as noncommercial, producing a hetero-geneous and nonstandardized product, and encouraging a creative process in which an individual creator works to achieve his or her personal ends more than those of an audience.

DIFFERENCES AMONG CULTURES

Systematic evidence to evaluate the three charges is scarce, but the differences between popular and high culture as economic institutions are smaller than suggested. To be sure, popular culture is distributed by profit-seeking firms that try to maximize the audience, but then so is much of high culture, at least in America, where government subsidies and rich patrons are few. Although much has been written about the intense competitiveness and cynical marketing ethos of Hollywood and Madison Avenue, a study of art galleries, magazines, and book publishers appealing to a high culture public would show similar features. Indeed, pressures to deceive the customer and to cut corners in relationships with competitors may be even more marked in some high culture firms, for example, in the art world, if only because their market is smaller, making it necessary to struggle harder to get business.

One major difference between popular culture and high culture is the size and heterogeneity of the total audience.[6] High culture appeals to a small number of people, probably not more than half a million in the whole country, whereas a popular television program may attract an audience of over 40 million. Because the popular audience is larger, it is also more heterogeneous, and although the high culture public prides itself on the individuality of its tastes, it is in fact more homogeneous than the publics of popular culture. Given the size of the audience, popular culture is often mass-produced, but so is much of high culture, for example, its books, records, and films. A few high culture users are rich enough to buy original paintings, but most, like the buyers of popular art, must be satisfied with mass-produced prints.

In order to produce culture cheaply enough so that people of ordinary income can afford it, the creators of popular culture, faced with a heterogeneous audience, must appeal to the aesthetic standards it holds in common, and emphasize content that will be meaningful to as many in the audience as possible. Whether the resulting culture is, however, more homogeneous than high culture can be questioned. Popular culture is more standardized, making more use of formulas, stereotypical characters and plots, although even high culture is not free from standardization. For example, many recent "serious" novels have made the theme of the artist as a young man, borrowed originally from Joyce and D. H. Lawrence, into a formula, featuring a stereotypical young man striving to develop his identity as an artist. Westerns may resemble each other more than high culture drama of a similar genre, but Westerns are as different from family comedies as high culture drama is from high culture comedy. Conversely, the differences within a given genre are no smaller in popular culture than in high culture; there are as many varieties of rock as of baroque chamber music, even though scholars only study—and thus publicize—the variations in the latter. Likewise, formal and substantive differences abound in popular art, although they are less visible than those in high art, which are discussed by critics and classified into schools by academics. In many ways, the different schools in high culture are equivalent to the different formulas in popular culture, for both represent widely accepted solutions to a given creative problem.

Since each taste culture is sensitive only to its own diversity and judges the others to be more uniform, a careful comparative study would be needed to say whether there is actually more diversity in high culture than in popular culture. The same observation applies to the amount of originality, innovation, and conscious experimentation. Both cultures encourage innovation and experimentation, but are likely to reject the innovator if his innovation is not accepted by audiences. High culture experiments that are rejected by audiences in the creator's lifetime may, however, become classics in another era, whereas popular culture experiments are forgotten if not immediately successful. Even so, in both cultures innovation is rare, although in high culture it is celebrated and in popular culture it is taken for granted. High culture being more timeless than popular culture, its classics are constantly revived for contemporary audiences, but since the late 1960s, when nostalgia began to be profitable, popular culture classics have also been revived, usually in modernized forms.

DIFFERENCES AMONG CREATORS

Finally, the differences between the motives, methods, and roles of the creators are also fewer than has been suggested.[7] A number of studies have indicated that creators are communicating with an audience, real or imagined, even in high culture, and that the stereotypes of the lonely high culture artist who creates only for himself or herself, and of the popular culture creators who suppress their own values and cater only to an audience, are both false.[8] Many popular culture creators want to express their personal values and tastes in much the same way as the high culture creator and want to be free from control by the audience and media executives. Conversely, "serious" artists also want to obtain positive responses from their peers and audiences, and their work is also a compromise between their own values and those of an intended audience. Some high culture creators, particularly those working on a freelance basis, may put their own values before that of the audience, and accept a smaller audience in the tradeoff, whereas many popular culture creators, at least those who are employees, must produce for a large audience and cannot make this tradeoff. (Whether these reactions are functions of culture or of occupational

23

position within the culture-producing agency remains to be studied.)

Even so, popular culture creators also try to impose their own taste and values on the audience, and many see themselves as popular educators, trying to improve audience taste. For example, when I interviewed some writers of popular television series several years ago, they pointed out that they were always trying to insert their own values into their writing, particularly to make a moral or didactic point. If and when producers objected—as they sometimes did—the end result was usually a compromise, for the producer cannot get along without the writer, and writers, like their high culture peers, are reluctant to compromise their own values.[9] In films and plays, where the production pace is more leisurely and the budget more flexible, the writer who cannot work out a compromise is replaced by another, and sometimes, several writers—and directors—are employed before the film or play opens. In high culture, on the other hand, creators who cannot produce for an audience are simply ignored, and their product vanishes into museums, libraries, and scholarly studies.

One of the major reasons for the conflict between writers and producers has to do with the class and educational differences between popular culture creators and their audiences, which do not exist—or at least not as often—in high culture. Many popular culture creators are better educated than their audiences and are upper-middle-class in status, so that when they create, say, for a lower-middle-class audience, some differences in values and tastes are inevitable. Because creators are of higher status than their audiences, they try to impose their own tastes, but because the product they create must reach the largest possible audience, producers, whose jobs depend on the rating or the box office results, must stop them from doing so. When the audience for a given television series (or movie) is heterogeneous, for example in class or age, the writer's taste may appeal to part of that audience but not to another's, and much of the producer-writer conflict is over which part of the audience—or more correctly, the audience as they imagine it to be—is to be given priority. When the audience is more homogeneous, the gap between the creator and the audience—and the producer—is much smaller, and in many cases, creators share the tastes of their audience. Indeed, the most popular creators come from much the same socioeconomic and educational background as their audience and therefore share its taste, much like the real or idealized folk-artist who created folk culture for his audience. In high culture, the creator-audience gap is much smaller, if only because the audience is smaller, more homogeneous, and usually of the same educational and class background as the creator.

Nevertheless, some distance must always exist between creators and their audiences, because creators look at culture differently than its users. Creators make culture their work, whereas users do not, and can rarely have as much interest or ego-involvement in a cultural product as the person who created it. For creators, culture is often the organizing principle of their lives, whereas users are more likely to treat it as a tool for information or enjoyment. This difference between creators and users, which I shall discuss further below as creator-orientation and user-orientation, leads to different perspectives toward culture which exist in popular culture as well as high culture and are a more important cause of the alienation of the artist from the audience than value or taste differences between them.[10]

The critics of mass culture are creator-oriented; they argue that differences of perspective between creators and users should not exist because users must bend to the will of creators, taking what is given them, and treating culture from the creator's perspective. Whether users have any right to their own perspective, and to having that perspective affect the creation of culture is, of course, a question of values, and

25

as I shall argue in Chapter Two, they have that right, because culture cannot exist without them. A creator needs an audience as much as an audience needs a creator, and both are essential to the product.

Moreover, the freedom of the popular culture creator to ignore user perspectives is not as limited, and that of the high culture creator not as limitless as is often thought. In fact, a recent study of Hollywood studio musicians suggested that the men who perform the background music for the movies found their work more creative and their working conditions freer than when they played in symphony orchestras.[11] In all the mass media, creative people who are successful are generally free to do what they want or think is right, provided they stay within the acceptable formats and do not antagonize important elements in the audience, but this is also the case in high culture. Of course, successful creators are free in part because they have accepted, consciously or unconsciously, the basic goals and policies of the firms and institutions within which they work, and in both high and popular cultures, young innovators face many obstacles unless and until they can prove that their innovations will be accepted.

Actually, the freedom of the creators depends less on whether they are in high or popular culture than on whether they are working in an individual or group medium. A novelist can create a finished product by himself, but playwrights, filmmakers and musicians are inevitably involved in group enterprises, and their work is often changed by other group members who also participate in creating the finished product. Because it is older and intended for a smaller audience, high culture is more often communicated through the individual media, but artistic conflict between the playwright and the director is as likely in a high culture play as in a popular one. In popular culture, there may be more conflict over which sectors of the total audience are to be reached, but this is a function of audience size and heterogeneity; and when the occasional high culture work becomes popular, there is the same pressure on the creator to change it so as to attract the popular audience. Even so, popular culture creators fight as intensely for their own ideas as high culture creators, and thinking of the former as opportunistic hacks out to give an audience what it wants is an unfair and inaccurate surrender to a facile stereotype.

Popular Culture's Danger
to High Culture

The second theme of the mass culture critique includes two charges: that popular culture borrows content from high culture with the consequence of debasing it; and that, by offering economic incentives, popular culture is able to lure away potential high culture creators, thus impairing the quality of high culture. Van den Haag describes his conception of the process:

Corruption of past high culture by popular culture takes numerous forms, starting with direct adulteration. Bach candied by Stokowski, Bizet coarsened by Rodgers and Hammerstein. . . . Freud vulgarized into columns of newspaper correspondence advice (how to be happy though well-adjusted). Corruption also takes the form of mutilation and condensation . . . works are cut, condensed, simplified and rewritten until all possibilities of unfamiliar or esthetic experience are strained out. . . . [12]

Although it is fair to ask what is wrong about cultures borrowing from each other, popular culture does borrow from high culture. The reverse is also true, however, for jazz and folk music have been borrowed by high culture composers; folk myths, by high culture playwrights; folk building styles by high culture architects; and "primitive art" by high

27

culture artists as well as audiences. In the past, high culture borrowed only from folk art, especially after the folk had lost interest in it, but as folk art became extinct, high culture has had to borrow from its commercial successor. Serious composers now borrow melodies from popular culture in the same way as their predecessors borrowed from folk music, and in the 1960s Oldenburg and others borrowed freely from the comic strips and commercial art. Perhaps popular culture takes more from high culture than vice versa, but partly because its audience is larger and requires more cultural production; if high culture had to satisfy the same quantitative demand, it might borrow more from popular culture than it now does.

When a high culture product, style, or method is taken over by popular culture, it is altered, but this also happens when popular arts are taken up by high culture. When an item of high culture is borrowed, however, the high culture public may thereafter consider it tainted because its use by the popular culture has lowered its cultural prestige. Popular culture audiences, on the other hand, may be pleased if their fare is borrowed from or by a culture of higher status.

To understand properly the charge of debasement, one must distinguish between effects on the creator and effects on the culture as a whole. Undoubtedly, high culture creators suffer when they see their work changed, but so do popular culture creators, even though only the former call it debasement. There is no evidence, however, that borrowing has led to a debasement of high culture per se, or of its vitality. The creation of high culture continues and I do not know of any high culture creator who has stopped working because his previous creations were taken over by popular culture.

The charge that popular culture lures away potential high culture creators is accurate, although some creators who have made money in popular culture are also lured into high culture by its prestige. Still, the high culture creators who earn a living in popular culture need not therefore be less creative in high culture.[13] This charge can only be tested, however, if they have a chance to spend all their time on the latter. More important, it is not at all clear that there would be more high culture if the pay scale of popular culture were not so tempting; not every high culture creator can work in popular culture. For example, few high culture writers can write for popular audiences, as the failure of serious novelists in Hollywood has repeatedly demonstrated.

Even so, the vitality of high culture would not necessarily be increased if popular culture stopped luring potential high culture creators. Given the present size of the high culture audience for music, concert violinists would still have no more opportunity to play, and more high culture novelists would only reduce the already small sales of individual novels. Adding to the number of high culture creators would increase competition between them, but whether this would add to high culture vitality is questionable. If popular culture did not exist, high culture creators would have to earn their living in other than cultural pursuits; violinists could not earn a living by playing in Broadway or Hollywood studio orchestras, and they might actually have less time to play and practice if they had to hold nine-to-five jobs. Serious writers lack such opportunites, however; like T. S. Eliot, they have often had to take fulltime editorial jobs in publishing houses.

If one looks at high culture from a strictly economic perspective, it may be described as a low-wage industry which loses some of its workers to high-wage competitors and hopes that the rest will be satisfied with the spiritual benefits of low-wage and high-status employment. Given the affluence of the rest of society, the spiritual benefits that once were attractive no longer suffice, however. The rising financial expectations of high culture creators can be met only by raising their incomes, and not by eliminating popular culture. A more effective solution would be to tax highly profitable cultural enterprises in order to subsidize unprofitable but socially desirable ones.

Popular Culture's Impact on Its Audience

A third—and far more serious—theme of the mass culture critique accuses popular culture of producing harmful effects on the people who use it. A number of specific effects have been postulated: that popular culture is emotionally destructive because it provides spurious gratification and is brutalizing in its emphasis on violence and sex; that it is intellectually destructive because it offers meretricious and escapist content which inhibits people's ability to cope with reality; and that it is culturally destructive, impairing people's ability to partake of high culture. For example, MacDonald describes popular culture as "a debased, trivial culture that voids both the deep realities (sex, death, failure, tragedy) and also the simple spontaneous pleasures. . . . The masses, debauched by several generations of this sort of thing, in turn come to demand trivial and comfortable cultural products."[14] Van den Haag puts it similarly:

All mass media in the end alienate people from personal experience and though appearing to offset it, intensify their moral isolation from each other, from reality and from themselves. One may turn to the mass media when lonely or bored. But mass media, once they become a habit, impair the capacity for meaningful experience. . . . The habit feeds on itself, establishing a vicious circle as addictions do. . . . Even the most profound of experiences, articulated too often on the same level (by the media), is reduced to a cliche. . . . They lessen people's capacity to experience life itself.[15]

The harmful effects charge is based on three assumptions:

that the behavior for which popular culture is held responsible actually exists and is widespread; that the content of popular culture contains models of such behavior; and that it therefore has negative effects. These assumptions are not supported by the available data.

THE EFFECTS OF POPULAR CULTURE

To begin with, there is no evidence that the vast number of Americans exposed to popular culture can be described as atomized, narcotized, brutalized, escapist, or unable to cope with reality. These descriptions are difficult to translate into empirical measures, which is why they can be bandied about loosely, but the overall picture that can be put together from sociological research, particularly community studies, is that most people are not isolated atoms, but are members of family, peer, and social groups, and that, within these groups, they tend to be moral, kind, pragmatic, and sometimes remarkably altruistic. In situations of stress, however, and when faced by outsiders who are or are considered threatening, they can be quite unfeeling and even brutal. Studies among the poor suggest that among the very poor, some (but not all) are socially isolated, depressed, and even narcotized, given to pathologies that can be escapist or brutalizing, and retreating into addiction or serious mental illness rather than coping with reality.[16] There is also some evidence that the poor use the mass media more and more intensely than others and that they trust it more,[17] but research into the causes of mental illness suggests fairly unequivocally that the constant stress, crisis, and insecurity that accompany poverty are responsible.[18] Moreover, poor people have been the victims of high rates of pathology for centuries, long before popular culture was invented, and indeed, during the time the folk art celebrated by the critics flourished.[19]

The fact that most Americans and even most poor people do not behave in the ways critics say they do could be used to invalidate the harmful effects charge from the outset, but there is no doubt that the content of popular culture has some of the characteristics attributed to it by these critics. Consequently, one must determine the effects of that content. The evidence from a generation of studies of the effects of various mass media suggests, however, that the media do not have the simple Pavlovian impact attributed to them, and that the critics' practice of inferring effects from content is not valid. Rather, media content is one of many stimuli which people choose and to which they respond in a number of ways—and which, in fact, they help to create through the feedback they exert on the mass media in the first place.

Several studies have shown that people choose media content to fit individual and group requirements, rather than adapting their life to what the media prescribe or glorify. They are not isolated individuals hungering for and therefore slavishly accepting what the media offer them, but families, couples, and peer groups who use the media when and if the content is relevant to group goals and needs.[20] Thus the audience cannot be considered a mass.[21] Moreover, people pay much less attention to the media and are much less swayed by its content than the critics, who are highly sensitive to verbal and other symbolic materials, believe. They use the media for diversion and would not think of applying its content to their own lives.[22] Even adolescents who are loyal fans of teenage performers do not model themselves or base their choice of dates and spouses on these performers, press agent claims nothwithstanding. Finally, content choice is affected by selective perception, so that people often choose content that agrees with their own values and interpret conflicting content so as to support these values. Thus the prime effect of the media is to reinforce already existing behavior and attitudes, rather than to create new ones.[23]

In recent years, most effects research has concerned itself

with the impact of television violence, particularly on children. While the 1969 review of the available evidence by the staff of the National Commission on the Causes and Prevention of Violence concluded that television reinforced and legitimated violence, it hesitated to suggest that television had a direct and significant causal effect; on the other hand, the 1972 Report of the Surgeon General's Advisory Committee, based on studies it had commissioned, suggested that there might be a correlation between television viewing and aggressive behavior.[24]

Nevertheless, my reading of the existing research suggests that the media encourage violent attitudes and acts only for some people at some times. To be sure, laboratory studies have long shown that violent films stimulate aggressive impulses and actions among youthful subjects immediately afterward, but no one has yet been able to demonstrate persuasively that a long-range effect persists. Studies outside the laboratory have found some correlations between television violence and aggressive behavior, but none have been able to demonstrate that television was the cause. Nor is it likely that they can, for real-life aggression is usually the result of group conflict which often arises spontaneously, and unless children have watched television immediately prior to the conflict, it is hard to imagine either that television has caused it or that it has shaped the aggressive expression of the conflict. Television and other media simply do not play that large a role in most children's lives; the actions and attitudes they learn from parents and peers are far more important. "Loners" may resort to aggression partly because they do not belong to any group and because they find substitute satisfaction in media fiction and other sources of fantasy, and there is some evidence that emotionally disturbed children and adults are affected by media violence, as are people predisposed to violent acting-out.

If the media had as significant an effect on aggressive

behavior as the critics and some researchers charge, a constantly increasing tide of violence should have manifested itself in America since the emergence of the mass media, but historical studies suggest that violent crime has declined over this period.[25] In addition, girls and the nonpoor should be as violence-prone as boys and the poor, for they watch the same media fare in about the same amount, but the effects studies show consistently that girls do not react aggressively after watching media violence, and police records continue to indicate that violence is much greater among males and among the poor. Moreover, poverty bred violence even before the mass media were invented. Thus, it seems prudent to hypothesize that media violence has particular impact on low-income boys and men, but that the prime cause of that impact is to be found in their living conditions, in which violence is commonplace, rather than in the media.

America is in many ways a violent society, permitting all kinds of violence against foreigners, minorities, and deviants, which is duly reflected and publicized by factual and fictional media fare. But the predominant cause of that violence is the inequality of American society which, exacerbated by population heterogeneity, creates social conflicts, and these in turn are often resolved by the use of force on the part of participants in the conflict—and by the police. Consequently, even if all the media agreed to ban all violent fare, I doubt that rates of violence would decrease significantly.

Similar conclusions can be reached about the media's effect on sexual behavior. Undoubtedly erotic films arouse people sexually for a while, but this may be beneficial and is certainly not harmful, since it does not lead to sex offenses. Research conducted for the Commission on Obscenity and Pornography showed once again that no long-range effects, harmful or therapeutic, follow from the use of erotica, and the Danes discovered that ending the laws against pornography did not lead to an increase in sex crimes.[26] In fact, if the media had any significant impact on sexual norms, the contemporary liberalization of sexual attitudes and behavior could not have taken place, for the media have been until recently quite Puritan, lagging far behind attitude changes among the younger audience for fear of alienating the older audience. If media audiences practiced what the media have preached, the double standard would still be in force, young girls would be virginal teasers, and adultery would be found only in the suburbs.

These observations about media violence and sex apply to other criticized elements of popular culture as well. By any objective measure, popular culture features many happy endings, heroes with supernatural moral and other virtues, and contrived solutions to insoluble problems, among others. Objective measurements of content do not, however, measure the meanings which audiences give to what they see or read, and these meanings are often different from those of the critics. Nor is there any persuasive evidence that such content leads to undesirable effects. For example, van den Haag argues that the media offer "substitute gratifications,"[27] but few people seem to use the media for problem solving, or media fiction for descriptions or explanations of reality, so that they do not take media content at face value. They use the media to provide temporary respite from everyday life, and fantasy serves this purpose better than realism.[28]

Still, unknown numbers of children and adults are unable to make the crucial distinction between the make-believe of popular culture and the reality of their own lives, although a rarely cited study by Freidson points out that children are trained in what he calls "adult discount" before they are ten.[29] Unknown numbers of children and adults are also taken in by the puffery and exaggeration of advertising, and ought to be protected against it; but part of the attractiveness of the ads is that people want the offered goods and it is not

35

at all certain that the ads themselves initiate the wants. Nor is it wrong that people should want things that are useful or provide pleasure. Moreover, studies of advertising impact and the complaints of advertising executives suggest that most people retain little of the ad content they see and misinterpret much of the message. Successful ads produce sharp increases in sales curves, but often these reflect the behavior of only a few hundred thousand people, and no one yet knows the relative impact of ad and product on buying decisions.

THE EFFECTS OF NEWS

The effects of news coverage have never been studied properly, although there is some evidence that the news media provide more news than the majority of the audience is willing to accept;[30] that viewers are not particularly devoted even to their favorite network news program; and that people project their own political attitudes on their favorite television newsman.[31] Older studies of the effects of propaganda and documentary films showed that they changed few attitudes,[32] and even though the national news media all reported the police riot which took place during the 1968 Democratic convention in Chicago, opinion polls made shortly afterward indicated that most respondents nevertheless sided with the police against the demonstrators. Voting studies made twenty years ago concluded that at that time, few people made up their minds on the basis of media reports—or campaign speeches—and studies of the 1960 Nixon-Kennedy television debates came up with a similar conclusion.[33] Since then, party loyalty has decreased, however, more voters are undecided or independent, and political candidates use a good deal of political advertising, mainly on television, to try to influence them. Although political television commercials have not always been effective—in the 1968, 1970, and 1972 elections, many of the candidates who campaigned mainly on television lost—even an impact on a very small proportion of the electorate can be significant when elections are won by a miniscule margin, as is increasingly the case.

The use of political advertising is harmful mainly when competing candidates—or issues—have unequal resources and the affluent ones can dominate the media. The fault lies less with the media, however, than with economic inequities which can be used to political advantage, and the inability of the public to protect democratic institutions against the holders of great economic power.

Most of the impact of the news media probably results from the news rather than from political advertising, and from the way that the news is presented. Some mass-communication researchers now argue that the primary effect of the news media is "agenda setting," that the media report the news about which political debate takes place, or as Steven Chaffee puts it, "mass communication serves more to determine the questions than it does the answers that people consider in reaching their political decisions."[34] Needless to say, however, the news media do not set the agenda in a vacuum; they choose what they report from the events that have actually happened, from what the sources of news to which they have access or which have access to them provide, and from their own perception of what they think is "newsworthy."[35] Although journalists aim to be objective in gathering the news, economic, technical, and aesthetic considerations influence the selection of the stories they cover and report, as do their own professional and personal values. For example, because journalists consider it their role to report fully on the activities of the president—partly because it is one of the few types of news that is thought to interest all of the national audience—they give more publicity to him than to his opponents, or to the pressure groups which influence his activities. Vietnam news normally described the

North Vietnamese as the enemy, an ethnocentrism that most journalists expressed unintentionally, even though the North Vietnamese were not the news media's enemy. And while journalists attempt to be fair and present a "balanced" description of controversial issues by reporting "both sides," they are more likely to mention Democratic and Republican sides than socialist or conservative ones.

In the last few years, journalists have become increasingly aware of their intentional and unintentional biases, partly because of criticism from both the Left and the Right. Still, it is not possible for them to be unbiased, for the very selection of newsworthy stories from the billions of events that take place every day requires the application of values, and besides, journalists are themselves members of American society. In conceptualizing, researching, and analyzing the events they describe, they cannot help but do so from the perspectives of their society, or at least of their profession, class, and age-group, among others, and from the values and interests associated with these.

The effect of the journalists' own values—and of the way they judge what events are newsworthy—on the audience is probably smaller than is generally thought, for with respect to events and issues about which people care deeply, they rely on more personal sources of information—and bias. The media may be more influential on perceptions of events and issues about which people care less, particularly outside the United States. For example, the media probably helped to perpetuate the Cold War by their hostile or unsympathetic coverage of events behind the Iron Curtain. Although they did not initiate American anticommunism by their coverage, they reinforced it, but then the journalists themselves shared the country's hostility to communism, and even if they had not, the businessmen who run the news media and are for political and economic reasons strongly opposed to communism, would have replaced them with journalists who shared their own biases.

The main impact of the news media is probably indirect; that is, journalists help to create the picture of the society and the world on which they report. Politicians and other societal decision makers not only see this picture but also try to determine how public opinion will react to it, which then influences their subsequent decisions. In addition, the news media, simply by covering the events they consider newsworthy, give publicity—negative or positive—to some issues, groups, and leaders, and not to others, thus allowing them to try to influence the audience. Indeed, the news media—and the mass media generally—can be viewed as a communication channel which the various interest groups and subcultures of American society try to fill with news which presents their viewpoints positively and those of their opponents negatively, and whoever gains the most access to this channel wins the chance to at least try to influence the audience. Access to the news media is, however, unequally distributed; groups which can generate a lot of news stories, like the federal government, or those which can hire press agents have greater access than the unorganized and nonaffluent parts of society. Thus, the poor rarely have access to the news media to present their viewpoints on major issues unless they riot, and this is one reason they sometimes riot.

THE EFFECTS DATA SUMMARIZED

The overall effects of the mass media—for news, other information, and entertainment—may be summarized as follows. So far, it is difficult to attribute any large-scale permanent effects of specific items or types of media content, although it seems likely that the media may have negative effects on media "addicts," people whose entire emotional and cognitive life is centered almost entirely on the media, and others predisposed to pathology who find their behavior publicized by media content. (Conversely, there are also people whose life is limited to high culture and devoid of human relationships, and although their pathology is no different, it is not blamed on high culture.) Finally, children and the poorly educated, both of whom make extensive use of the media and may be less skilled in the uses of "discount" that come with adulthood and education, may be more affected by the media than the rest of the population.

No one can deny that the media may have ill effects on some people, but this is true of all institutions in society, including the family, and so far there is no evidence that the social and other costs of the media outweigh their benefits. It is, of course, possible to argue that any institution which harms only a few or creates cost only for some ought to be eliminated, but this argument is impractical, and if it is held consistently, would require the elimination of society in entirety. Interestingly enough, some critics who wish to banish the media and popular culture for their harmfulness seem much less interested in banning other phenomena which are actually much more harmful, including war and poverty.

It should be noted that all of the available studies of media effects measure conscious effects and say little or nothing about possible unconscious ones. Moreover, they deal with the short-range impact of a few specific types and items of content, and have not properly considered the effects of the settings in which specific types of content are set, or of the medium per se. For example, there have been many studies of the effects of violence in films and television, but few of the differential effects of the various kinds of characters who are violent, and even fewer of the effects of the overwhelmingly middle-class settings and populations of most entertainment fare on poor people. Nor has anyone attempted to compare the effects of a movie musical and a stage musical or a vaudeville show, although there have been some studies of the educational utility of different media.

Marshall McLuhan argues that the content of the media is less important than the media themselves—that these media are the message—and has speculated that television has retribalized society and is making the world over into a global village. McLuhan is only partly accurate, however, for while television's emphasis on moving pictures and its resulting de-emphasis of words and of intellectual analysis can be traced in part to television as a medium, a shortage of analysis also exists in the printed media, and is probably due more to the audience's lack of interest in analysis than to the nature of the media. Television has also increased people's knowledge of life in other countries, but the "globalization" of the world is better explained by the rising economic and political interdependence of all countries than by the introduction of television, while the retribalization of some parts of society has more to do with the need for alternatives to the nuclear family now that its economic functions have disappeared and some of its emotional dysfunctions are becoming visible.

Finally, no one has yet been able to study the effects of living in a society in which the mass media are so important. In the past, no one thought to compare societies before and after the invention of the radio and the movie, and in recent decades, many opportunities were missed to compare societies before and after they adopted television. The effects of the media per se are probably greater than of individual media, and those of the earlier media are probably greater than those of later ones like television, but even if the introduction of modern media could still be studied among the few societies currently without them, the basic question may be unanswerable because the arrival of the media cannot easily be isolated from the many other changes such a society undergoes at the same time. In most instances, the media are introduced concurrently with many other consumer goods and "modern" institutions.

Nevertheless, there is no doubt that the media have had an effect on society. They have, for example, speeded up the demise of folk cultures, because commercial popular culture is almost always more attractive to people than their folk culture. They have also provided much more information to people about their own society, by describing, both through fact and fiction, the different life-styles, aspirations, and attitudes currently coexisting in the society. Not only have the media made societies more aware of their pluralism, but because they have almost always emphasized middle-class culture and attitudes, they have probably aided in the diffusion of middle-class culture and increased its cultural as well as political power. Although the decline of working- and lower-class cultures in America must be explained by other factors as well, the mass media have played their part by their virtual exclusion of these cultures from their offerings.

Whether the many effects of the media have in sum been more beneficial than harmful, or vice versa, is deserving of study, but even so, the question is almost irrelevant today, because it is impossible either to eliminate these media now, or even to conceive of a large modern society existing without them. The mass media are here to stay, and the more significant question is to ask whether they need to be improved, and if so, how.

Debate about media effects will continue as further studies shed additional light on them, but meanwhile, at least one conclusion about their effects can be suggested: that a sizeable difference exists between the media effects postulated by the critics of mass culture and those discovered by empirical research. As a result, it would appear that the critics are making unwarranted inferences about the extent, intensity, and harmfulness of media effects; because they dislike media content and popular culture generally, they come to it with the aesthetic standards of high culture and are shocked by what they see, hear, and read. Since they assume that the media audience shares—or ought to share— their standards, they naturally project their own reactions on the audience. The same process occurs, however, when people who prefer popular culture come into contact with high culture; they are frequently shocked by its espousal of "deviant" behavior, especially on the part of the artist, and they condemn it in terms similar to those in the mass culture critique. For example, during the 1960s, cultural and political satire was often called "sick comedy," and Lenny Bruce was hounded off the stage and into suicide by the police and the courts. The defenders of high and popular culture attack each other in many ways. High culture condemns popular culture as vulgar and pathological, while popular culture attacks high culture for being overly intellectual, snobbish, and effeminate, inventing pejorative terms like "highbrow" and "egghead" for this purpose. There is some difference in methods of attack, however; whereas high culture expresses its disapproval of popular culture mainly in books and literary journals, popular culture publics also use the police, the pulpit, and the political arena to attack their enemies.

The weapons used by popular attackers of high culture are far more powerful, of course, but otherwise, the process is the same. In both instances, advocates of one culture view the other with different standards, disapproving of what they find, and expressing their disapproval by alleging harmful effects on the audience. Why they do this, why their standards differ, which standards are the right ones, and how this affects the evaluation of high and popular culture will be discussed in Chapters Two and Three.

Popular Culture's Harmfulness to Society

The critique of popular culture's effects on society contains two charges. One argues that popular culture lowers the taste level of society as a whole, thus impairing its quality as a civilization. A second suggests that because the mass media can "narcotize" and "atomize" people, they render them susceptible to techniques of mass persuasion which skilled demagogues can use to abrogate democracy.[36] Bernard Rosenberg summarizes these charges: "At its worst, mass culture threatens not merely to cretinize our taste but to brutalize our senses while paving the way to totalitarianism. And the interlocking media all conspire to that end."[37]

A broader statement of the second charge, often identified with the New Left but also voiced on the Right, is that mass culture is inimical to democracy. As Herbert Marcuse sees it, the corporate control of modern technology has led to a society in which popular culture makes people more and more comfortable with their life while robbing them of their freedom to oppose what is in reality an evil social system which tolerates poverty, wages imperialistic war on innocent peasants, and permits internal dissent only as long as it remains ineffective.[38] Jacques Ellul, a French conservative, also sees modern technology as the major villain. He argues that technology leads to mass society, and if it is democratic, it requires citizens to participate in politics. Because ordinary people cannot, however, cope with the mass of information and other knowledge required for proper citizenship, they need what Ellul calls propaganda, a mixture of facts, values, and advocacy statements, including both the intentional propaganda of the State and other powerful institutions and the unintentional propaganda of mass culture. Intentional propagandists are, of course, only too ready to provide information which advocates and advances their interests, and Ellul concludes that, as a result, citizens become unwitting victims of the propagandists, and democracy is emasculated.[39]

CULTURE AND TASTE LEVELS

I believe that both of the societal charges against popular culture are inaccurate. The argument that popular culture leads to a societal decline of taste levels is based on a skewed comparison, with the best features of the past compared to the worst of the present.[40] Writers such as Oswald Spengler and Jose Ortega y Gasset remember only history's Shakespeares and Beethovens and forget their less talented colleagues whose work has been lost or ignored. Similarly, they recall selected kinds of folk art, but forget others that were more brutal or vulgar than anything in today's popular culture. By any comparison that draws from a representative historical sample and takes into account the majority of people in past and present societies, however, there has been a steady rise in the level of taste, especially in the last few decades, when the proportion of people going to college increased sharply. Although statistics about the rising number of classical record buyers and book club members may not prove that Americans are becoming cultured, they do suggest a significant change in taste from the pre-World War II days when even semiclassical music was considered highbrow.

In response, the critics argue that taste levels would be even higher if popular culture did not exist, but there is no evidence to back up this argument. In fact, the attempt of communist governments, especially in Eastern Europe, to discourage popular culture and to promote an official high culture have not been successful, and they have had to give in to the public demand for domestic versions of Western popular culture.

CULTURE AND TOTALITARIANISM

The charge that popular culture can lead to totalitarianism is based on the argument that with the increasing centralization of society, and what Karl Mannheim calls its "functional rationalization," the family and other primary groups and voluntary associations and other secondary groups that stand between the individual and the State are losing strength, leaving the individual as a powerless atom vis-à-vis the State.[41] If a demagogue can take over the mass media, he can use techniques of mass persuasion like those allegedly now employed by media advertisers to persuade individuals to accept dictatorship.[42] This argument is supported by the effectiveness with which Hitler and Stalin used their control over the mass media to maintain their totalitarian rule.

This analysis needs to be broken into constituent elements. It is true that the State can take over the society's mass media for its own goals; it may happen in wartime even in democratic societies. It is doubtful, however, that popular culture has the power to destroy small institutions and other sources of opposition. As I suggested previously, the media have not impaired the family or the peer group, and voluntary organizations in America have grown in number and in strength even during the most rapid growth of the mass media, not because of the influence of the media but because of the expansion of the middle class, which is active in such groups.

Even so, the power of the State is increasing, and under conditions of crisis it is possible that people will become fearful and panicky, or so threatened by social change that they are willing to give power to a strong leader who can promise to solve their problems. This inclination could be found among followers of the late Senator Joseph McCarthy and it exists today, particularly among right-wing and segregationist groups anxious about the possibility of more economic and racial equality, as well as among radical groups fearful of the use of State power against them. If enough people wanted or supported a strong leader, he or she might gain control of the mass media, especially if he or she promised economic or social relief to media owners or to media audiences. But here, too, the role of the media would be no different from its present one, the reinforcement of existing social trends. Thus, if major portions of the audience were in favor of dictatorship, they could easily force the media to provide content in its support, but the inability of the mass media to influence voting behavior on a large scale suggests that the media could not persuade their audiences to accept dictatorship. Popular culture can become a tool of dictatorship but by itself cannot materially contribute to the establishment of a totalitarian government.

Of course, one could and should ask whether the mass media ought to reinforce existing social trends, or whether they should be a bulwark against such dangers as totalitarianism. It would be easy to assign them the latter role, but illusory to expect them to carry it out. They could play a bulwark role only if they could ignore or cut themselves off from the audience when it is inclined toward totalitarianism; or if they could, as institutions, be strong enough to stand outside society and to repel it when it becomes undemocratic. Institutions which can stand outside society are hard to find, however, or even to conceive. The media cannot help but be a part of society, although they can do their share to preserve democracy if they are free to communicate all kinds of political content, including controversial ideas held by only a minute or powerless segment of the society, and if they can remain free of dominance or undue pressure by political and other interest groups.

Because the media help to shape the cultural and political climate of society, they are constantly beset by such pressure, and even by attempts to take them over. This is particularly true of television. In many European countries, television is controlled by the government, but such control is not desirable, for even when governments are democratic, they are less interested in advancing democracy than in staying in power. In America, television and the other media are controlled by commercial institutions, which are more interested in maximizing profits than in political control— except when media content becomes too critical of free enterprise. Even so, they are likely to support the media's democratic role only as long as it supports their profit-seeking, and when they or their advertisers become antidemocratic, the media's democratic role is restricted. As commercial firms, the media are, however, freer from political pressure than they would be under government control; even though American television is in some respects regulated by government through the Federal Communications Commission, it has been able to defend itself against much—though not all—of the pressure that now emanates from the federal government, especially the White House. In a democratic society, the ideal solution would be to have the media organized as nonprofit institutions which can remain isolated from governmental, commercial, and other pressures, but it is precisely such institutions which are hard to find or conceive. Public broadcasting, though a nonprofit institution, has sometimes been even less successful than the commercial television networks in defending itself against pressure from government, or from the business and "civic" leaders who sit on its policymaking boards.

The Marcusian analysis does not concern itself with how popular culture or the media actually function; it is an argument in behalf of Marcuse's own vision of an egalitarian democracy, based on the proposition that all institutions—including the media—which are not devoted to achieving his vision of democracy are by definition undemocratic and ought to be suppressed. Thus, Marcuse favors "the withdrawal of toleration of speech and assembly from groups and movements which promote aggressive policies, armament, chauvinism, discrimination . . . or which oppose the extension of public services, social security, medical care, etc."[43] Unfortunately, Marcuse reserves to himself the right to define democratic and antidemocratic "groups and movements," and to determine therefore who is to be suppressed and who is entitled to his or her own opinion.

For Marcuse, popular culture is dangerous not only because it is harmful to its users, but also because it "narcotizes" them to accept the political status quo. Marcuse thus goes beyond other critics of mass culture to suggest that enjoyment of popular culture might discourage people from overthrowing the existing political and economic order. He is even opposed to the current liberalization of sexual norms and practices because it too diverts people from the revolutionary role he assigns them.

Unlike other mass culture critics, Marcuse argues in behalf of the politically oppressed, and points out correctly that prevailing forms of dissent, civil liberties, tolerance (and culture) are so institutionalized that they cannot change the political system—and in fact only make powerful groups stronger because they can rule without abrogating dissent and civil liberties. However, since he defines the oppressed as just about everyone except the corporate and political elites and withholds the right of the oppressed to determine their own destiny (and culture), his critique can best be understood as a revolutionary statement in which the only role of culture is to hasten the coming of the revolution. Marcuse may be accurate that culture—including both popular and high— diverts people from acting politically, although its ability to divert is miniscule in comparison with, for example, the family, but he is wrong to assume that people would become revolutionaries if the present culture were replaced by a revolutionary one. Just as the mass media do not change behavior and attitudes significantly, a revolutionary culture will not make its users into revolutionaries, particularly if that culture is imposed by a revolutionary elite. Moreover, even in revolutionary times, not all people join the revolution, and even those who do still need the diversion that culture provides. Until one can determine to what extent popular culture causes or encourages public support of war, poverty, racism, chauvinism, and so forth, and whether people would be more willing to do away with these evils if popular culture were abolished or altered, it is impossible to consider popular culture as a counter-revolutionary tool even if one were to accept Marcuse's goals.

Whereas Marcuse's analysis is flawed by his unwillingness

to accept any culture which is not revolutionary, Ellul's is flawed by his overly broad definition of propaganda. Ellul is right to point out that when people are flooded with the ephemeral and often contradictory information that emanates from news media, they can easily become confused, then are likely to accept that information which fits their preconceptions, and thus are prone to fall victim to propagandistic statements in line with these preconceptions. Nevertheless, Ellul's overall argument is unpersuasive, and on two grounds. First, if all popular culture is propaganda, then the term propaganda becomes meaningless, and Ellul is reduced to arguing that all culture has undemocratic consequences and that modern society cannot be democratic. Whether or not modern society can be democratic depends in large part on how one defines democracy, and Ellul's pessimistic answer follows directly from his definition, because for him democracy exists only when autonomous individuals who are immune both to propaganda and social pressure can form their own opinions and then public opinion. This definition rests on an asocial conception of human beings and of opinion formation, however, and the autonomous individuals he favors do not exist in the real world. Ellul implies that they—and therefore democracy—did exist in the past, but his failure to demonstrate their existence with historical data reduces his implication to romantic nostalgia. In other words, Ellul sets up unachievable criteria for democracy, then finds society to be undemocratic, and therefore blames propaganda and culture. Like other mass culture critics, Ellul sees no positive features in modern society, and perceives ordinary people as robots who succumb to propaganda like Pavlov's dogs—and these two themes, which run through all his books, fatally distort his more specific arguments.

Second, while Ellul's indictment extends to all modern societies, most of his examples of the dangers of propaganda are taken from Nazi Germany, Soviet Russia, and France (a country in which the State has considerable control over the news media), but he does not sufficiently analyze England and the United States, where these media often exist in an adversary relationship to the State. By Ellul's broad definition, they also offer up propaganda, but it is very different both in intent and content from Nazi or Soviet propaganda, and can thus provide information for public opinion that opposes the State. In fact, in America, journalism has historically viewed itself as a self-appointed exposer of political sin, and as in the Watergate scandals, can debunk State propaganda and reduce the power of the State. Ellul may be correct in arguing that all mass communication, whether intentional propaganda or not, consist of statements of advocacy in behalf of one or another cause or value, but that does not mean they are either undemocratic by definition or will necessarily have totalitarian consequences.

The Sources and Biases of the Mass Culture Critique

When compared to the available empirical and other evidence, the mass culture critique does not stand up well. Not only are there similarities in how popular and high culture are created, but the former poses no genuine threat to high culture or its creators. Moreover, popular culture content does not have the effects attributed to it, except perhaps on a minority of people who consume it in other than the accepted ways. Because of its lack of overall effect, it cannot be considered a source of danger to the society or to a democratic form of government.

Consequently, the critique is largely a statement of aesthetic dissatisfaction with popular culture content, justified by an incorrect estimate of negative effects and based on a false conception of the uses and functions of popular culture. Before embarking on an analysis of both high and popular culture, I want to discuss why the critique exists and what its major biases are that make it inappropriate.

THE POLITICAL FUNCTIONS OF THE CRITIQUE

At one level, the critique is a plea for an ideal way of life guided by the humanist dictates of high culture that emerged during the Enlightenment and by the standards of humanist thinkers who place a high value on personal autonomy, individual creativity, and the rejection of group norms. These standards are undoubtedly conducive to the creation of high culture, but whether they ought to guide everyone and be applied on a society-wide basis is open to question. This question will be discussed in Chapter Three. At another level, however, the critique is also a plea for the restoration of an elitist order by the creators of high culture, the literary critics and essayists who support them, and a number of social critics—including some sociologists—who are unhappy with the tendencies toward cultural democracy that exist in every modern society. The analysis of the political function of the critique requires a brief exploration of the history of popular culture and its critique.

During the preindustrial era, European societies were divided culturally into high and folk culture. The latter was sparse, homemade, and, because peasants lived in isolated villages, largely invisible. The former was supported by the city-dwelling elites—the court, the nobility, the priesthood, and merchants—who had the time, education, and resources for entertainment and art and were able to subsidize a small number of creative people to produce culture for them. Both artists and intellectuals were close to the sources of power and some shared the prestige and privileges of their employers and patrons. Because of the low social status and geographical isolation of folk culture, they also had a virtual monopoly on public and visible culture.

When economic and technological changes forced the peasants into the cities and gave them the free time and disposable income for their own art and entertainment, they shed the rural-based folk culture and became customers for a commercial popular culture that soon outnumbered in quantity the products and creators of high culture, and eventually destroyed its monopoly position as the only public and visible culture. As the economic resources and power of the rich patrons decreased, the creators of high culture were forced to leave the court society and look for support and audiences elsewhere. Eventually, they had to compete with popular culture in what might be called "the culture market."

These changes could only seem undesirable and threatening to many of the creators of what was now explicitly described as high culture. The decline of the court reduced their prestige, their source of support, and their privileges. The rise of a huge market for the popular arts meant for them not only a severe reduction of cultural standards but also a loss of control over the setting of standards for publics of lower status and education. In this process the artists forgot the subordination and humiliation that they had often suffered at the hands of their patrons, and failed to appreciate the freedom and dignity that they acquired even as they lost their guaranteed audience and its economic support. They solved the problem of their audience by denying that they needed one; they created only for themselves and their peers who could appreciate their work. Consequently, they had only contempt for the new publics on whom they depended for economic support, even though these offered artists greater rewards and more freedom than they had had before. The cult of the artist as genius, later transformed into the romantic image of the artist, provided culture with the prestige it lost when it was no longer associated with the aristocracy.[44]

The creators of culture thus experienced a considerable and rapid change of status and power and some were faced with drastic downward social mobility. Among their elite patrons, this downward mobility led to the development of reactionary political and social movements, but among the artists and intellectuals it produced an ideology of *ressentiment* expressed not only in novels and other content that bemoaned the passing of the old order, but also in the formulation of the mass culture critique.

Since the conditions which initially evoked the critique were European, most of the critics have also been European, or Americans who were descendants from the European elite or who modeled themselves on it. (As I noted in the Introduction, there was also a homegrown American version of the critique, however, which took the form of a crusade against liquor, sex, and later vaudeville and movies, with elite WASP Americans condemning the poor, particularly those coming from Europe, for not living up to their Puritan standards. This critique was never fully developed intellectually, but appeared in reform and anti-immigrant political writing of the late nineteenth and early twentieth century.)

The writers who contributed to and disseminated the critique in recent decades came, for the most part, from two political camps. One group consisted of conservatives, for example Jacques Ellul, T. S. Eliot, F. R. Leavis, and Jose Ortega y Gasset in Europe, and Ernest van den Haag and Russell Kirk, among others, in America. A second group of critics I shall call socialists, although they represented a particular point of view within Marxist ideology and not all of them consider themselves socialists or Marxists today. The major European writers of the Left were associated with the Frankfurt School, among them Theodor Adorno, Max Horkheimer, Leo Lowenthal, and Herbert Marcuse; the major American writers included Clement Greenberg, Irving Howe, Dwight MacDonald, Bernard Rosenberg, and Harold Rosenberg.[45] The socialist criticism of mass culture was in some ways similar to that of the conservatives, although it was not hostile to political democracy or to social and economic equality.

The socialist critics also diverged from the conservatives in their analysis of the causes of the problem of culture. The conservatives explained the existence of popular culture by the inadequacy of its audiences; the socialists pointed out that mass society and the use of the market mechanism to provide culture were at fault, and that these led to the destruction of folk culture and its replacement by a new commercial popular culture which people did not want but which they could neither prevent nor resist. The conservatives attacked popular culture because they resented the rising political, economic, and cultural power of the so-called masses; the socialists, because they were disappointed that these masses, once liberated from proletarianism, did not accept high culture or support socialist advocacy of it.

Despite their differing explanations of the rise of popular culture, the two groups were both fearful of the power of popular culture, rejected the desirability of cultural democracy, and felt impelled to defend high culture against what they deemed to be a serious threat from popular culture, the industries that provide it, and its publics.[46]

THE HISTORICAL BIAS OF THE CRITIQUE

The same conditions that led to the development of the mass culture critique also produced its major biases. The first is what I call the historical fallacy: a regressive and pessimistic view of the historical process, which postulates a continuing decline of the quality of life since the replacement of the small cohesive community and its folk culture by urban-industrial society and its popular culture. Such pessimism is not unusual among downwardly mobile groups, for they exaggerate their own loss of influence into a theory of overall social deterioration. However, all the evidence suggests that the good old days were hardly good, and the critics' view of the past is closer to historical fallacy than analysis.

This view of history begins with a romantic picture of a happy peasantry creating and enjoying folk culture, and is forced to underemphasize that many peasants lived under subhuman conditions, exploited by feudal landlords and merchants and enduring hunger, pestilence, and random violence as an everyday occurrence. As the quality of their lives deteriorated further with the beginnings of urban-industrial society, one response was folk culture with more violence and brutality than is even imaginable by the critics who consider today's popular culture to be violent. Bearbaiting, visits to the lunatic asylum to taunt the mentally ill, attendance at public executions and widespread drunkenness were staple items in the folk culture of early urban-industrial society.[47] The folk culture of yet earlier, agrarian societies was less brutal, except in its treatment of outsiders and foreigners, but still, it was hardly as benign as the nostalgic critics imply.

Actually, studies of people in transition from so-called folk society to modern society suggest that many of the charges laid against contemporary society really apply to preindustrial and early industrial societies, but become inaccurate when these societies have achieved greater affluence. The nostalgia about the solidarity and "community" of folk society notwithstanding, people in both preindustrial and early industrial societies were often apathetic, submissive, atomized individuals considered incapable of holding opinions about their welfare. Lacking this right, the power to defend themselves, and the vote, they were subject to restrictive group pressures and domination by secular and religious elites.[48]

Only in a modern industrial society have ordinary people

begun to be liberated from these oppressions. The affluent ones among them have become, in Daniel Lerner's phrase, members of a participant society in which they can hold opinions and, if the society is democratic, begin to affect their own destinies. (The irony is, however, that just as people are able to participate more, the increasing complexity of society encourages a centralization of functions and power that reduces the ability of individuals to affect the society through their participation.) Moreover, thanks in part to the availability of education, ordinary people have been enabled to begin to think of themselves as individuals, to develop themselves as such, and to want the values of autonomy and individual creativity which the humanists advocate. As Edward Shils puts it:

A new order of society has taken form since the end of World War I in the United States. . . . This new order of society, despite all its internal conflicts, discloses in the individual a greater sense of attachment to the society as a whole, and of affinity with his fellows. . . .

The new society is a mass society precisely in the sense that the mass of the population has become incorporated *into* society. The center of society—the central institutions and the central value systems which guide and legitimate these institutions—has extended its boundaries. Most of the population (the "mass") now stands in a closer relationship to the center than has been the case either in premodern societies or in the earlier phases of modern society. In previous societies, a substantial proportion, often the majority, were born and forever remained "outsiders."[49]

Popular culture has played a useful role in the process of enabling ordinary people to become individuals, develop their identities, and find ways of achieving creativity and self-expression. Popular culture has not caused these changes; it has only helped predisposed people to achieve them by providing examples and suggesting ideas. For example, in their content, the mass media have always been stalwart defenders of individualism and personal freedom; a large proportion of the Hollywood films of the pre-television era portrayed individual heroes who liberated themselves from parental authority and learned to act on their own, even if their actions were often violent or extralegal.[50] The movies which dealt with or idealized the life-styles of the middle and upper classes provided role-models which helped the immigrants to become Americanized and middle class, and they gave poor people, as they still do, a picture of what life was like without poverty. Even though the media have probably not created aspirations for upward mobility—these aspirations develop among poor people through sheer deprivation and relative deprivation alone—they have helped to flesh them out. The soap operas of radio, film, and television have supplied housewives with information about how to solve their own problems; even if the problems of the soap opera characters have often been sensational or exotic ones not often encountered by their audiences, they have provided the message that people, as individuals, could solve their own emotional and social problems through their own efforts and the right kind of information. Popular dramas and melo-dramas, including Westerns, have dealt with and resolved an immense variety of moral and ethical problems, even if the context was historical or fantastic, and many episodes in today's television series are about such issues as racial discrimination, intermarriage, tolerance toward deviant be-havior, and the like. The issues are rarely presented as they appear in ordinary life, and problems are solved much too easily, but still, they offer ideas to the audience which it can apply to its own situation. The homemaking and house-and-garden magazines encourage their readers to be creative and to achieve aesthetic satisfaction, even if their furnishings require more money than people have.

It is possible (and easy) to criticize the soap operas for not dealing with more typical problems, and the homemaking magazines for not featuring less expensive designs, but it is also possible that their current users would then reject them. No one has yet tried a socially realistic soap opera or a financially realistic homemaking magazine, at least in the last generation, and while both might be successful, the fact that they have not been tried over this period also suggests that they might not be successful. Perhaps their users want some fantasy in both.

The critics scoff at popular culture as offering only spurious gratification and misinformation, but they do not view that culture from the same perspective as the audience. The critics assume that the audience is or ought to be as highly educated as they are, that it is already used to individualism and individual problem solving, that it has been socialized and educated to strive for creativity and self-expression, that it has the expertise to solve problems directly and rationally, and that it has no need for escape or entertainment. Although the critics overestimate their own culture's orthodoxy—high culture also offers escape and spurious problem solving—they have little understanding of the way in which life is lived in Middle America. Many working and even middle-class Americans are still in the process of liberating themselves from traditional parental cultures and learning how to be individuals with their own needs and values. For example, for a housewife who has decided that she wants to decorate her home her own way, rather than in the way her parents or neighbors have always done, the homemaking magazines provide not only a legitimation of her own striving toward individual self-expression but an array of solutions from various taste cultures from which she can begin to develop her own.[51] Similarly, the spate of women's liberation articles in popular women's magazines helps a woman still deeply immersed in a male-dominated society to find ideas and feelings that allow her to start to struggle for her own freedom.

It could be argued, however, that at the time ordinary people were shedding the restrictive patterns of folk culture and feudalism, they could have been encouraged to participate in high culture, thus doing away with the need for popular culture. However, high culture was inaccessible to them. The social and political elite that supported high culture not only rejected popular participation in elite activities generally, but made no effort to provide the rest of society with the economic and other prerequisites needed to share in high culture. Until the twentieth century upper income groups were frequently opposed to educating lower ones, for they were fearful that literacy would only lead to revolution and the loss of their privileges.

Today, this opposition is minimal, but now, the users of popular culture are often described as being conditioned to accept nothing else by decades of mass media fare. Whether they are so conditioned is an empirical question which no one has answered, although there is historical evidence to suggest that the content of the mass media was borrowed to some extent from earlier popular cultures and even folk cultures. Today's popular culture did not come into being with the invention of the radio and the moving picture, but is as old as high culture, and is therefore not simply the result of a conditioning process.

Even so, data on the socioeconomic and educational backgrounds of high culture publics suggest that it is not popular culture which prevents people from participating in high culture, but the absence of the prerequisite background, and the lack of opportunity for obtaining it. If more people had access to high incomes and a quality liberal arts education, many present devotees of popular culture would be able to participate in high culture, and at least some of them would be willing to do so. This hypothesis and its policy implications will be considered again in Chapter Three.

OTHER BIASES OF THE CRITIQUE

The historical fallacy shores up two other biases. One is a marked disdain for ordinary people and their aesthetic capacities, illustrated by the previously noted belief that the media have a Pavlovian hold on their audience and can persuade it to accept any emotion or idea they wish. The critics' low opinion of the popular culture audience and the role it plays in their critique has been tellingly noted by Shils in a statement that summarizes in two paragraphs the essential fault of the critique:

The contention has been made frequently that mass culture is bad because it serves as a narcotic, because it affects our political democracy, because it corrupts our high culture. I don't think there is any empirical evidence for these contentions and what impressionistic evidence there is does not support them either. I think we are not confronting the real problem: Why we don't like mass culture. . . . It is repulsive to us. Is it partly because we don't like the working classes and the middle classes?

Some people dislike the working classes more than the middle classes, depending on their political backgrounds. But the real fact is that from an esthetic and moral standpoint, the objects of mass culture are repulsive to us. This ought to be admitted. To do so would help us select an esthetic viewpoint, a system of moral judgments which would be applicable to the products of mass culture; but I think it would also relieve our minds from the necessity of making up fictions about the empirical consequences of mass culture.[52]

A second bias stemming from the historical fallacy is the assumption that the entire output of today's high culture must compare favorably with what has survived of past high culture, and that it must come up to the standards of what are today interpreted as golden ages of high culture, such as Periclean Athens, Elizabethan England, and the Renaissance. Such comparisons forget, of course, that most of the ordinary people of these societies lived in poverty (or even slavery), and that directly or indirectly they contributed to the support of an elite that could in turn support high culture. Since this comparison judges the quality of society by the quality of its (surviving) high culture, the critics are implying that the major goal of society is to assure the creation of the best high culture possible, and that all other goals, such as the general welfare, are secondary.[53] In essence, then, the mass culture critique is self-serving, oriented to the interests of high culture alone, and to the maximization of its power and resources. High culture advocates are as entitled as anyone else to be self-serving, but they have no right to mask their self-interest as the public interest, or to suggest that society as a whole ought to be organized around the effort to advance the fortunes of high culture.

The final bias of the popular culture critique follows directly from the preceding—what I call its *creator-orientation*. As I suggested earlier, any item of culture may be evaluated from two perspectives—that of the creator and that of the user. The former views culture as existing for the people who create it, rejecting any attempt to satisfy an audience; the latter looks at culture from the point of view of its users, and asks to what extent culture is meeting their wishes and needs.

High culture is creator-oriented and its aesthetics and its principles of criticism are based on this orientation. The belief that the creator's intentions are crucial and the values of the audience almost irrelevant functions to protect creators from the audience, making it easier for them to create, although it ignores the reality that every creator must respond to some extent to an audience.

The popular arts are, on the whole, *user-oriented*, and exist to satisfy audience values and wishes. This is perhaps the major reason for the antagonism of high culture toward the popular arts and the tone of the mass culture critique. High culture needs an audience as much as popular culture, but it is fearful that the audience will be wooed away by a user-oriented culture or that it will demand what might be called its democratic-cultural right to be considered in the creative process of high culture.

As a result, high culture needs to attack popular culture, and especially its borrowing of high culture content, because borrowing transforms that content into a user-oriented form. Moreover, high culture needs to think of popular culture as of low quality, of its creators as hacks, and its audience as culturally oppressed people without aesthetic standards. If high culture is to maintain its creator orientation, it must be able to show that only *it* is guided by aesthetic standards, and that only *its* creators and audiences are complete human beings, and that for these reasons it has a right to maintain its cultural status and power. The irony is that to defend its creator orientation it requires status, and to claim such status it must compare itself to something lower. This is one reason why the mass culture critique continues to exist.

In short, that critique is partly an ideology of defense, constructed to protect the cultural and political privileges of high culture. Like all such ideologies, it exaggerates the power of its opposition and the harmful consequences that would follow from permitting this opposition to exist. Yet even if high culture has lost its monopoly on culture and has had to give up some of its privileges and power in the cultural marketplace, its continuing vitality in an age when the popular arts are also flowering suggests that the defensive portions of the ideology are not as necessary for high culture as the critics believe. This portion of the ideology is also undesirable, for it seeks to protect high culture and its creators at the expense of the rest of culture and society. In this process it conjures up false dangers and spurious social problems, making it impossible to understand the popular arts or to evaluate them properly.

In the remaining chapters, I will develop an alternative way of looking at high culture and popular culture that accepts both and makes it possible to arrive at what I consider a more useful evaluation of both.

CHAPTER TWO

A Comparative Analysis of High and Popular Culture

A comparative analysis of high and popular culture must begin not with personal judgments about their quality but with a perspective that sees each of them as existing because they satisfy the needs and wishes of some people, even if they dissatisfy those of other people.

I start with the basic assumption that all human beings have aesthetic urges;[1] a receptivity to symbolic expressions of their wishes and fears; a demand for both knowledge and wish-fulfillment about their society; and a desire to spend free time, if such exists, in ways that diverge from their work routine. Therefore, every society must provide art, entertainment, and information for its members. People may be their own creators, or they may simply recruit someone to function temporarily as a creator, or they may turn, as in modern society, to trained fulltime creators.

Moreover, a society's art, information, and entertainment do not develop in a vacuum; they must meet standards of form and substance which grow out of the values of the society and the needs and characteristics of its members. Thus the aesthetic standards of every society can be related to other of its features, and one can expect a tribe of hunters to have concepts of beauty, art, and leisure different from those of today's factory workers or intellectuals. Homogeneous societies offer little cultural diversity; they generally develop only a single concept of beauty, one style of art (often religious), and one way of home furnishing. American society, with its pervasive division of labor and heterogeneity, includes varieties of art ranging from pinups to abstract expressionism, types of music ranging from the latest rock hit to electronic chamber music, and most important, an equally large number of aesthetic standards to determine the choices people make from the available content.

These choices are not made randomly. Research into consumer behavior and leisure indicates that choices are related; people who read *Harper's* or the *New Yorker* are also likely to prefer foreign movies and public television, to listen to classical (but not chamber) music, play tennis, choose contemporary furniture, and eat gourmet foods. Subscribers to the *Reader's Digest*, on the other hand, probably go to the big Hollywood films if they go to the movies at all, watch the family comedies on commercial television, listen to popular ballads or old Broadway musicals, go bowling, choose traditional furniture and representational art, and eat American homestyle cooking. And the men who read *Argosy* will watch Westerns and sports on television, attend boxing matches and horse races, and let their wives choose the furniture but prefer the overstuffed kind.[2]

These relationships between choices exist because the choices are based on similar values and aesthetic standards, or at least on similar choices between the lesser of two evils when no cultural products which express these values are available. The values and standards constitute the basis of what I defined earlier as a *taste culture*, and the people who make similar choices for similar reasons are a *taste public*. Different taste cultures and taste publics exist because of the diversity of and disagreement about aesthetic standards and values. For example, while there may be agreement about the desirability of visual order in art, there is disagreement about how order is to be defined, and what constitutes order and disorder in art. The visual order of a de Kooning painting is interpreted as disorder by lower taste cultures, and the visual order of calendar art is not considered art by high culture.

Because each taste public has somewhat distinctive standards, every major taste culture has its own art, music, fiction, nonfiction, poetry, films, television programs, architecture, favored foods, and so forth; and each culture has its own writers, artists, performers, critics, and so forth. Each culture also has its own institutions for meeting people's aesthetic needs. Although all Americans consume art, high culture publics select their art from original oils and "quality reproductions," often in galleries, whereas other publics choose mass-produced originals and reproductions, bought at department store art counters; and the very poor may have to rely on calendars and magazine pictures which they hang on their walls. Similarly, the universal demand for drama is satisfied for some publics mainly by the legitimate theater, for others by movies and television, and for yet others by football games and wrestling matches.

This comparative approach thus rejects the dichotomy of high and popular culture and the idea that the former maintains aesthetic standards while the latter exists for nonaesthetic reasons. Moreover, instead of assuming a single popular culture, I propose that the number of cultures is an empirical and a conceptual problem, to be determined in part by studies of who chooses what content and what relationships exist among content choices. The idea of a number of taste cultures is not new; it has been expressed in literary and popular writings by the conception of cultures and publics as highbrow, middlebrow and lowbrow.[3] I call this idea *aesthetic pluralism.*

Taste Cultures
and Publics

Taste cultures are not cohesive value systems, and taste publics are not organized groups; the former are aggregates of similar values and usually but not always similar content, and the latter are aggregates of people with usually but not always similar values making similar choices from the available offerings of culture. Moreover, they are analytic aggregates which are constructed by the social researcher, rather than real aggregates which perceive themselves as such, although at times people who make up a taste public do act as a group, for example, to protest the cancellation of a favorite television program or to defend high culture against an external threat. Analytic aggregates can have boundaries because they are demarcated by the researcher, but these boundaries are also analytic artifacts.

Many factors determine a person's choice among taste cultures, particularly class, age, religion, ethnic and racial background, regional origin, and place of residence, as well as personality factors which translate themselves into wants for specific types of cultural content. Because ethnic, religious, regional, and place differences are disappearing rapidly in American society, however, the major sources of subcultural variety are increasingly those of age and class.[4] Young people are the main carriers of innovation, at least in every changing society; and if they do not invent new cultural items, they flock to them, partly to express their separation from other age groups and their cohesion as an age group, but also because in Western society they are a leisure class, at least if they are affluent, and they require innovation, if only because they require so much cultural fare.

Nevertheless, the major source of differentiation between taste cultures and publics is socioeconomic level or *class.*[5] Among the three criteria that sociologists use most often to define and describe class position—income, occupation, and education—the most important factor is education (by which I mean, here and elsewhere, not only schooling but also what people learn from the mass media and other sources), and for two reasons. First, every item of cultural content carries with it a built-in educational requirement, low for the comic strip, high for the poetry of T. S. Eliot. Second, aesthetic standards and taste are taught in our society both by the home and the school. Thus a person's educational achievement and the kind of school he or she attended will probably predict better than any other single index that person's cultural choices. Since both of these are closely related to an individual's (and his or her parents') socioeconomic level, the range of taste cultures and publics follows the range and hierarchy of classes in American society, although the correlation is hardly perfect.

Consequently, I shall describe five taste publics and their cultures, labeling them with terms adapted from the Warnerian conception of class-culture. Although stylistically poor, these terms have the advantage of being relatively neutral, as long as high is not judged positively and low negatively, but I use them here as neutral categories, favoring neither higher nor lower, and judging none as being more or less desirable or aesthetic.[6]

The five publics and cultures to be described are called *high culture*, *upper-middle culture*, *lower-middle culture*, *low culture*, and *quasi-folk low culture*.[7] The choice of five cultures is somewhat arbitrary, however, and different analytic purposes would result in different numbers. For example, the making of cultural policy would require greater specificity and many more publics and cultures would have to be identified.

In addition, the descriptions to follow have a number of limitations. *First*, they are about general American cultures and leave out ethnic, religious, regional, and other variants within them—although ethnic cultures are discussed briefly in a subsequent section. Moreover, every taste public is stratified by age, but my descriptions will deal mainly with adult publics and their cultures—although the so-called youth culture will also be discussed briefly in a subsequent section.

Second, the descriptions exaggerate the extent to which cultures and publics are cohesive and bounded systems, and I must note once again that they are analytic rather than real

71

aggregates. As a result, the descriptions also overemphasize the boundaries between cultures and publics; in the real world, many items of culture can be classified as being part of two cultures, and may in fact be shared by two publics. Moreover, some people regularly choose from more than one culture and thus can be classified as being in more than one public. Also, publics and cultures will be treated as relatively homogeneous and static wholes, even though in reality each has many subgroupings, including factions that might be called traditional, conventional, and progressive (or academic, establishment, and avant-garde, as they are sometimes referred to in high culture). Undoubtedly age correlates strongly with these factions, the progressives being younger than the traditionalists.

Third, I shall describe publics and their cultures rather than the reverse, because the characteristics of publics are better known and their standards are relatively stable. Cultures change over time, and specific fashions more often, partly because taste culture is used for leisure and people seem to want variety, partly because changes in the society have their reverberations in culture. Indeed, culture change has accelerated in recent years and the pace by which a progressive cultural form becomes conventional and is replaced by a new progressive form has quickened, particularly in high culture art.[8] In popular culture, change is also endemic, although it seems to be cyclical, for movies and television programs go through "cycles" of short duration. One year, television Westerns gain the highest Nielsen ratings, only to be replaced by detective mysteries, or by family comedies, and then again by Westerns.

Even so, the changes in these programs are often of a type David Riesman has described as marginal differentiation, and the popular television fare of the 1970s is not much different from that of the 1950s, or of the "B" movies of a yet earlier era. The plots and characters of television and films have become more complex and dialogue more sophisticated, but many of the contemporary reincarnations of the 1950s television family comedy "Ozzie and Harriet" continue to feature the smart wife and not-so-smart husband. Perhaps the most important change has been in the relative size of the various taste publics, for as a result of rising incomes and educational levels, low culture has declined, and upper-middle and lower-middle culture have grown quantitatively and qualitatively.

Fourth, the description of cultures and publics does not apply my earlier distinction between creator and user orientation, except in the case of high culture. A fuller analysis would have to identify both orientations for each culture. Not only do the fulltime creators in every culture have different perspectives than their audience, but in that audience, many people are also amateur creators, particularly through their hobbies or avocations. In such activities, they will act on the basis of creator-oriented standards, which vary from the standards they apply as users. Thus, a high culture user of classical music who also paints may judge music from a user perspective but art from a creator perspective. A lower-middle culture television fan who also builds hot rods will be like his peers in his television preferences, but he will reject the user-oriented standards of the same peers who buy Detroit's sedans. The hot rod builder will probably not, however, step outside the standards of his own taste culture in designing his car; on the outside, it is likely to resemble a current Detroit model rather than the sleek European racing car body favored by an upper-middle or high culture car buff.

Fifth, I should note that I am here describing what might be called *lay* taste cultures, those which create content for the general public, and I am ignoring what might be called *professional* taste cultures, which exist in many professions and scientific disciplines. Sociology, for example, includes a high culture of grand theorists, with functionalist, Marxist, and other factions, as well as one that builds such theory out of mathematical models; a low culture to which sociological popularizers who write only for the lay audience are relegated; and several middle cultures made up of the textbook writers and the researchers who conduct the small-scale empirical studies that fill the professional journals. Even this description is overly simple, for it leaves out the research administrators who carry out large empirical studies and the majority of sociologists who do little or no research at all.

The humanities differ from other disciplines in that there is considerable overlap between professional and lay high culture. The former is created by academics; the latter partly by scholars but mostly by the nationally and internationally known writers and other creators who are freelancers or occasional artists-in-residence in the academy. A good deal of technically difficult creative work which would be considered professional in other disciplines is part of lay high culture, on the assumption that the high culture public is or ought to be so well-educated that it can read technical criticism in literature. As a result, narrow and abstruse literary writing will appear in a lay high culture journal, but equally narrow and abstruse social science writing will not, because the lay public is not expected to understand it, and because of high culture's preference for literary analysis and its disdain for most social science research.

Sixth, the taste cultures will be described in terms of their most widely distributed products, particularly the commercially distributed ones, so that I am emphasizing the commercial portions of the cultures at the expense of the rest. The analysis ignores altogether the cultural fare many people still create at home and in the community, whether as art, entertainment, or information, or for that matter, as myth and ceremony. Some of this fare is local adaptation of the national commercial culture, as when a community group honors one of its officers by performing a homemade version of "This Is Your Life" for him or her, or when children or adults compose erotic or sacrilegious versions of currently popular songs. Much of the noncommercial culture is, however, either original or adapted from earlier folk culture, for example, children's games and the music created by occupational groups, such as the work and protest songs of miners.

Seventh, my descriptions of the six publics and cultures are mere thumbnail sketches which are brief and overly simple, particularly in characterizing the taste cultures, even though it is presumptuous to describe any taste culture—and not only high culture—in a few paragraphs. Moreover, these sketches are by no means complete; they emphasize a few selected components of the cultures which lend themselves to comparison across the cultures. Thus, I touch on the fiction and art of individual cultures, but leave out almost everything else. Finally, these sketches are so general that they cannot be used to classify individuals or individual cultural items, and they do not offer methodological guides or social and cultural indicators for classifying people or content into particular taste publics and cultures. Ethnological analyses of the various taste cultures are sorely needed, but I do not pretend to make them in the section to follow.

The Five Taste Publics
and Cultures

HIGH CULTURE

This culture differs from all other taste cultures in that it is dominated by creators—and critics—and that many of its users accept the standards and perspectives of creators. It is the culture of "serious" writers, artists, and the like, and its public

75

therefore includes a significant proportion of creators. Its users are of two kinds: (1) the creator-oriented users who, although not creators themselves, look at culture from a creator perspective; and (2) the user-oriented, who participate in high culture but are, like the users of other cultures, more interested in the creator's product than in his or her methods and in the problems associated with being a creator. Even so, the creators and both kinds of users are similar in one way: they are almost all highly educated people of upper and upper-middle class status, employed mainly in academic and professional occupations.

The culture itself is in some ways more of an aggregate than the other taste cultures. For example, it contains both classic and contemporary items which are formally and substantively diverse but are part of high culture because they are used by the same public. Thus, the culture includes simple lyrical medieval songs and complex formalistic modern music; "primitive" art and abstract expressionism; *Beowulf* and *Finnegan's Wake.* (Other taste cultures also use the classics, but to a much lesser extent, and they concentrate on those which are more congruent with contemporary items.) In addition, high culture changes more quickly than other cultures; in this century alone, its art has consisted of expressionism, impressionism, abstraction, conceptual art, and many other styles. Indeed, the major unchanging features of the culture are its domination by creators and the elite social position of its users.

Even so, there are some stable elements in the culture that set it off from other cultures. Perhaps most important, high culture plays explicit attention to the construction of cultural products, such as the relationships between form, substance, method, and overt content and covert symbolism, among others, although the relative emphasis that high culture places on these varies over time. In recent decades, innovation and experimentation in form have particularly dominated high culture art and music and, to a lesser extent, its fiction and architecture, just as methodology has dominated the social sciences. The culture's standards for substance are less variable; they almost always place high value on the careful communication of mood and feeling, on introspection rather than action, and on subtlety, so that much of the culture's content can be perceived and understood on several levels. High culture fiction emphasizes character development over plot, and the exploration of basic philosophical, psychological, and social issues, with heroes and heroines of novels and plays often modeled on the creators themselves. Thus, much high culture fiction deals with individual alienation, and the conflict between individual and society, reflecting the marginal role of the creator in contemporary society.

High culture's nonfiction is basically literary; in the past it relied on novelists for its analyses of social reality, and on critics who content-analyzed novels for what they reported about society. Today, the culture relies more on essayists for its nonfiction, leading at least one critic to argue that the serious novel has lost its major function. Social scientists who live up to the culture's writing standards are also read, but as I suggested earlier, high culture is often hostile to the social sciences, partly because of their proclivity to jargon (although the equally technical language of literary criticism is rarely condemned for this reason) and partly because they refuse to accept literary observations and autobiographical impressions as evidence.

Since the culture serves a small public that prides itself on exclusiveness, its products are not intended for distribution by the mass media. Its art takes the form of originals distributed through galleries; its books are published by subsidized presses or commercial publishers willing to take a financial loss for prestige reasons; its journals are the so-called little magazines; its theater is now concentrated largely in

Europe, New York's Off-Broadway, and occasional repertory companies. High culture has still not entirely accepted the electronic media, but its movies are often foreign and are shared with upper-middle culture, and what little high-culture television exists is also shared with this culture and is shown on public television.

Due to its creator orientation, high culture awards more status to creators than to performers, and actors are viewed not as stars but as tools of the director and dramatist unless they can demonstrate that they have taken part in directing their own performance. Critics are sometimes more important than creators, because they determine whether a given cultural item deserves to be considered high culture, and because they concern themselves with the aesthetic issues which are so important to the culture.[9] They lead the debate on aesthetic issues and their differences of opinion often affect subsequent creative work. Film critics, for example, first developed the "auteur theory," which proposes that films are shaped almost entirely by their directors, and this theory has not only increased the status of those directors praised as "auteurs" but has encouraged other directors to enlarge their role in film making. Aesthetic disagreements between critics or creators are often institutionalized, leading to the formation of ideological subfactions. For instance, there are several schools of avant-garde film making and film criticism, reflecting differences in standards about appropriate content and techniques of filming as well as about the role of the director.

High culture's prime allegiance is to its own creator-oriented public, but it also perceives itself as setting aesthetic standards and supplying the proper culture for the entire society. Although this perception, which plays an important role in the mass culture critique, is exaggerated, high culture does perform at least one distinctive function for the larger society and for the other taste cultures. Because it is creator-oriented and because its creators are highly trained, the culture addresses itself to abstract social, political, and philosophical questions and fundamental societal assumptions more often, more systematically, and more intensively than do the other cultures. This is not to say that high culture deals with all fundamental questions and that lower cultures ignore them. Moral issues are constantly treated in popular entertainment fare and philosophical issues come up as well, typically exemplified in concrete cases. Conversely, high culture does not often address itself to prosaic issues like making a living, because such issues are not problematic for its public.

I noted previously that the high culture public can be divided into two types, creator-oriented and user-oriented. The creator-oriented public views high culture from the creator's perspective, but the user-oriented public, though drawing on the same culture, selects what satisfies it without placing itself in the creator's position, or to put it another way, without doing the "aesthetic work" that high culture creators demand from their audience. The members of this public are thus like members of lower taste publics, choosing culture for the feelings and enjoyment it evokes and for the insight and information they can obtain; they are less concerned with how a work of art is created, and they may not appreciate or understand the work as completely as the creator and the creator-oriented public. They choose from a culture created by and for "experts" but as amateurs.

This public is probably much larger than the creator-oriented one, and of higher income and status, for it includes some of the patrons of art, music, and poetry who subsidize the creation of high culture, and the collectors of art—and artists—who are looking for profit or status. In addition, this public includes highly educated professionals and managers and also high culture creators who are amateurs in fields other than their own.

Creators are sometimes apt to characterize this public as philistines and hangers-on, who, like the fans and groupies that surround rock stars, are more interested in the creators than in their work, but their reaction reflects in large part the intrinsic differences between creators and users which exist in all taste cultures. To be sure, some members of the user-oriented public are interested in the status that derives from high culture, but so are some creators.

The user-oriented public of course shares high culture with the creator-oriented one, but it tends to eschew the more technical criticism and academic scholarship which is important to creators and critics, and gravitates to the more easily enjoyed and understood parts of the culture. This public also pays more attention to creators than to critics, and sometimes relates to the former as fans, in the process making stars out of the better-known creators. Over the years, this method of reifying the artist has been applied to Thomas Wolfe, Ernest Hemingway, J. D. Salinger, James Baldwin, and Norman Mailer, among others, although in recent years Mailer has also become a journalist and essayist who appeals mainly to the upper-middle culture public.

Since the user-oriented public is large and affluent, the commercial distributors of high culture try to cater to it, and to find and even change high culture content that will appeal to its pocketbook. For example, in the mid-1960s, Susan Sontag advocated "camp" as a legitimate form of creator high culture, but it was quickly sold to—and taken up by—the user-oriented public because it enabled people to use high culture for entertainment.[10] The resulting popularization of high culture sometimes leads creators and the creator-oriented public to develop new outlets by founding new galleries and magazines such as the *New York Review of Books.* In fact, this process may even affect the content of high culture, because when innovators find that their work is becoming too popular, some may be motivated to move on—although others will cash in on their popularity. It may be more than coincidence that the rapid change in art during the 1960s, including pop art, op art, minimal art, photographic realism, and conceptual art came at a time when abstract expressionism was becoming popular among the user-oriented public. Although some of these innovations lent themselves to quick acceptance among the user-oriented public, avant-garde experiments in other high culture media have not become popular, such as French structuralist fiction, or atonal electronic music.

The user-oriented public does not choose all its culture from high culture, but neither does the creator-oriented public. Because high culture is "serious," people often obtain some of their entertainment from lower cultures, becoming sports fans, avid readers of detective stories or habitués of films and television programs they consider bad. Still, even these choices are not random; high culture sports fans are more likely to follow baseball or football than low culture wrestling, or to read the novels of Dashiel Hammett than those of Mickey Spillane. This pattern of "straddling" cultures is universal; the upper-middle public will also stray into the lower cultures, and conversely, members of the lower publics will make occasional visits to a museum or symphonic concert.

UPPER-MIDDLE CULTURE

This is the taste culture of the vast majority of America's upper-middle class, the professionals, executives and managers and their wives who have attended the "better" colleges and universities. Although well-educated, they are not trained as creators or critics, and like the user-oriented public of high culture, they are not creator-oriented, but unlike the latter public, they do not find high culture satisfying. They want culture and want to be cultured, but prefer a culture that is substantive, unconcerned with innovation in form, and

81

uninterested in making issues of method and form a part of culture.[11]

As a result, upper-middle verbal culture is far less "literary," and art and music are much less abstract than is the case in high culture. Upper-middle fiction emphasizes plot more than mood and character development, although heroes and heroines are more important than in high culture. In content, upper-middle fiction reflects the permanent and current interests of its public, which in turn reflects that public's economic and other roles in society. For example, upper-middle culture audiences seem to prefer fiction about activities, ideas, and feelings relevant to their own endeavors, such as their careers and social and civic organizations. Since upper-middle users of culture—at least, the men—are economically and politically influential, their fictional heroes are more concerned with the ability to achieve their goals in competition (with others, bureaucracy, or nature) than with their alienation as individuals vis-à-vis the larger society. Consequently, they are drawn to novels, dramas, and biographies of individual achievement and upward mobility. Upper-middle women, I suspect, turn to fiction that depicts the struggle of women to compete with men in male-dominated enterprises, the problems of wives whose husbands are married to their work, and more recently, the potentialities and problems of women's liberation.

Since the upper-middle public is very much interested in how society—and society's leaders—work, I suspect that its use of nonfiction is comparatively greater than among all other taste publics. *Time* and *Newsweek* and other newsmagazines are written primarily for this public, as is the "New Journalism," the "nonfiction novel," and the popularized social science that appears in *Psychology Today* and in articles and columns of other magazines.

Upper-middle music includes the symphonic and operatic works of nineteenth-century composers, but excludes, with

82

some exception, the compositions of earlier centuries and contemporary music, as well as chamber music of all ages. Broadway musicals used to be written for the upper-middle public, but today this is only occasionally the case, although its younger members are probably the major consumers of folk music and the more melodic rock, as exemplified by *Hair*. A distinctly upper-middle art is harder to identify; I suspect that this public chooses what has become most popular among the user-oriented high culture public—with appropriate encouragement from the commercial distributors of art.

Even so, the upper-middle public shares relatively little culture with the high culture public, but it does borrow selected works, and it uses creators who began in high culture. For example, during the 1960s, upper-middle film-goers flocked to the lighter Ingmar Bergman films and made the Swedish director a star in their culture, but in recent years, as Bergman's work has again become more philosophical and pessimistic, he has lost much of this audience. Arthur Miller and Norman Mailer are among the creators who began their careers in high culture but have since changed or added publics, although not necessarily deliberately. As a result, the mass culture critics are especially hostile toward upper-middle culture—which Dwight MacDonald has called "Midcult"—because its public borrows from and sometimes alters high culture but refuses to join the high culture public.

The upper-middle public pays considerable attention to creators as "stars," and it relies extensively on critics and reviewers, who help it to differentiate between high and upper-middle culture content—and also between lower-middle and upper-middle content—when these are provided by the same media. Some but not all of the critics who review films, books, art, and music for the *New York Times* and upper-middle magazines carry out this function by disapproving of content which they perceive as too experimental or philosophical on the one hand, or too clichéd and "vulgar" on the other hand.

Upper-middle culture is distributed through the so-called class media or quality mass media. Its public reads the newsmagazines, *Harper's*, the *New Yorker*, *New York*, *Playboy*, *Ms.*, and *Vogue*, among others; it purchases most of the new hardcover "trade" books and thus helps to determine which are to be best-sellers; it supports the Broadway theater, although not as much as in years past, goes to see foreign film comedies and the "independent" productions that now come out of Hollywood. It provides the major audience for public television, network documentaries, and prestigious dramatic television specials, and also for museums and concert halls in the larger cities—and now in the suburbs.

Upper-middle culture is today probably the fastest growing of all taste cultures, the boom in college attendance having increased the size and affluence of the upper-middle public. Not only do many college students choose from this culture for their leisure activities, but they continue to do so afterward, resulting in the great popularity of foreign films, higher sales of trade books and the doubling of circulations among some "class" magazines during the 1960s. They have also supported the so-called youth culture to be discussed below. In addition, the young audience has encouraged the rise of a progressive upper-middle culture in which Vonnegut, Hesse, and Tolkien are major stars, but it has also affected conventional upper-middle culture, as suggested by changes in editorial policy in magazines like the *Atlantic* and the *New Yorker* to make them livelier and more "relevant."[12]

LOWER-MIDDLE CULTURE

Numerically, this is America's dominant taste culture and public today. It attracts middle- and lower-middle-class people in the lower-status professions, such as accountancy and public school teaching, and all but the lowest-level white-collar jobs. Although older members of this public have only a high school diploma, many of its younger ones have attended and graduated from state universities and the many small colleges that dot the American landscape.

This public is not particularly interested in what it calls "culture," by which it means both high and upper-middle culture, but whereas it was once opposed to the cosmopolitan sophistication of both cultures and even to their cultural institutions, this is no longer the case. Although it still dislikes abstract art and although it continues to reject most high culture and much of upper-middle culture, it now accepts "culture" and is already participating in cultural institutions which are seeking a larger audience and are willing to make the needed changes in their fare.[13] A number of museums have begun to exhibit well-designed consumer goods, art that comments on topical issues—for example, the Metropolitan Museum of Art's "Harlem on My Mind"—and artists who are, or once were, popular with the lower-middle public, such as Norman Rockwell. Some high and upper-middle art forms have been borrowed and adapted by illustrators and advertisers appearing in lower-middle magazines, and the movie and television industries adapt "serious" novels and dramas, or make television series out of upper-middle culture films like *M.A.S.H.*[14]

The aesthetics of lower-middle culture emphasize substance; form must serve to make substance more intelligible or gratifying. Dramatic materials express and reinforce the culture's own ideas and feelings, and although some questioning is permitted, doubts must usually be resolved at the conclusion of the drama. Its heroes are ordinary people, or extraordinary ones who turn out to be ordinary in that they accept the validity of traditional virtues, such as "wholesomeness," and traditional institutions, such as religion. For example, familial dramas deal primarily with the problem of upholding tradition and maintaining order against irrepressible sexual impulses and other upsetting influences. Unlike the two higher cultures, lower-middle culture rarely makes unresolvable conflicts explicit. Given its user-orientation, this public pays little attention to writers or directors, concentrating on performers. It prefers the word-of-mouth judgment of friends and neighbors to the views of formal critics, although it may listen to show business personalities when they act as informal critics.[15]

The lower-middle public provides the major audience for today's mass media; it is the group for which these media program most of their content. This public shares the newsmagazines with the upper-middle public but probably ignores its "back-of-the-book" cultural sections which are written for the upper-middle public; it used to read *Life*, *Look*, and the *Saturday Evening Post*, and makes possible the large circulations of the *Reader's Digest*, *Cosmopolitan*, other women's and homemaking magazines, and the many hobby magazines that have sprung up in the last two decades. It also supplies many of the buyers for popular novelists like Jacqueline Susann and Harold Robbins, who sell millions of copies of their books in paperbacks. Lower-middle audiences remain loyal to American films, although they may go to see only big musicals and other spectaculars; they are of course the viewers for whom television makes the situation comedies, popular dramas, and variety shows that record high Nielsen ratings.

The lower-middle public seems to be less interested in how society works than in reassurance that it continues to abide by the moral values important in lower-middle-class culture generally. Consequently, this public probably uses much less nonfiction than the upper-middle public (except for self-help and "how-to" content that aids people in solving personal problems and taking care of home, car, and other consumer goods). Instead, the lower-middle public reads novels and views films and television dramas that deal with fictional versions of recent world events and fictionalized biographies of important public figures and celebrities. Frequently, this content is a modern version of the morality play, in which characters sin and therefore come to an unhappy end, or renounce their evil ways and readopt the moral values of the lower-middle class. The novels of the Susann-Robbins genre are often fictional portraits of politicians, entertainers, corporate and show business executives (and other members of the upper and upper-middle classes) who finally realize that they ought to act—or ought to have acted—to uphold lower-middle-class morality. And while the lower-middle public rarely watches documentaries, it does watch entertainment programs which concern themselves with issues like racial tolerance, economic exploitation, or equal treatment under the law, particularly if these are set in a nonrealistic setting: in family comedies, detective stories or in the past, as in "Bonanza," the very popular Western series of the 1960s. Such content limits itself to social problems which are resolvable, or to social issues to which lower-middle-class moral standards can be applied unambiguously. Lower-middle culture does not often treat subjects in a manner that would disturb or upset its public, but then neither does any other culture, including high culture.

Lower-middle art continues to be mainly romantic and representational, shunning harsh naturalism as well as abstraction. Still, judging by the many stores offering quickly painted and inexpensive originals which have sprung up in the last decade, lower-middle publics are not only more willing and able to buy art than they were in the past, but are also ready to accept popular adaptations of nonrepresentational high and upper-middle culture art: imitations of cubists like Feininger in which the cubist method is altered in a more representational direction, and op art which is softened and romanticized by the use of pastel colors. Reproductions of the work of high culture artists can also be found in lower-middle outlets; for example, the landscapes of Cezanne and Van Gogh, the dancers of Degas, and the cityscapes of Buffet.

Today, lower-middle culture appears to be increasingly fragmented; differences among traditional, conventional, and progressive factions seem to be sharper than in other taste cultures. Much of the cultural conflict is over the treatment of sex; lower-middle traditionalists are still conservative about what they want to have depicted in public cultural fare, while the progressives are the constituency for the sexual frankness that appears today in *Cosmopolitan*, the Susann and Robbins novels, television documentaries about sexual problems, and, now, even television entertainment. For example, by 1972, impotence and abortion were treated in "All in the Family" and "Maude," and the unmarried heroine of the "Mary Tyler Moore Show" occasionally stayed out overnight, although her sex life was only hinted at.

Every narrowing of sexual and other taboos is protested by some audience members, but the protest appears to be limited to the more vocal traditionalists, while the large majority of conventional lower-middle-class people remain silent, and the upper-middle-class critics who review television fare applaud. Protest is widespread only when the taboos are relaxed for television and other fare which is watched by children, or when sex education is proposed in the schools, and perhaps the lower-middle public as a whole is altering its own sexual values but is sufficiently ambivalent about this alteration to want to shield its children from it.

Indeed, lower-middle culture may be changing as quickly as high culture, even if the change does not emphasize innovation of new forms so much as experimentation with adaptations of upper-middle culture. The rapidity of change has plunged some of the mass media creators and decision makers catering to this public into uncertainty; once-popular television series suddenly lose their audience and new ones never obtain one, and must be replaced by the end of the television year, or even in mid-season, at a faster pace than in the past. No one seems able to predict what this public wants or will accept, or more correctly, to find cultural fare that will appeal to all of its factions. The *Saturday Evening Post* and *Life* underwent a series of editorial policy changes in an unsuccessful attempt to find such fare, although their final demise was caused by their advertisers' preference for television rather than by significant audience dislike of the magazines.

LOW CULTURE

This is the culture of the older lower-middle class, but mainly of the skilled and semiskilled factory and service workers, and of the semiskilled white collar workers, the people who obtained nonacademic high school educations and often dropped out after the tenth grade. Low culture was America's dominant taste culture until the 1950s, when it was replaced by lower-middle culture. Its public, though still large, has been shrinking steadily, partly because of longer school attendance even among blue collar workers, but also because of the exposure to television and other lower-middle mass media on the part of young working-class people who have broken out of the isolation of urban ethnic and rural enclaves.

Low culture publics are still likely to reject "culture," and even with some degree of hostility. They find culture not only dull but also effeminate, immoral, and sacrilegious—which is why Spiro Agnew's caricature of upper-middle college students as "effete snobs" attracted so much attention—and they often support church, police, and governmental efforts to censor erotic materials. At the same time, their preference for action and melodrama, to be described below, explains their reluctance to support censorship of violence.

The aesthetic standards of low culture stress substance, form being totally subservient, and there is no explicit concern with abstract ideas or even with fictional forms of contemporary social problems and issues. As a result, high and upper-middle culture is almost never borrowed and adapted. Low culture also emphasizes the morality play, but it limits itself primarily to familial and individual problems and to values which apply to such problems; low culture content thus depicts how traditional working-class values win out over the temptation to give in to conflicting impulses and behavior patterns. The culture's dominant values are dramatized and sensationalized more than in lower-middle culture; the emphasis is on demarcating good and evil. Low culture fiction is often melodramatic and its world is divided more clearly into heroes and villains, with the former always winning out eventually over the latter.

Working-class society practices sexual segregation in social life: male and female roles are sharply differentiated, even within the family, although both differentiation and segregation are now declining.[16] These patterns are reflected in low culture, so that there are male and female types of content, rarely shared by both sexes. Sexual segregation and working-class values are well expressed in the Hollywood action film and television program—and of course in sports programming—as well as in the adventure magazines written for the male public, and the fan and confession magazines written for the female public.

The male action drama typically described an individual hero's fight against crime and related violations of the moral order, or his attempt to save society from a natural disaster, but in either case, the issues are always clear. For example, a lower-middle Western may tell the story of the conflict between ranchers and farmers, but a low cultural Western is more often about cowboys fighting criminals or outlaws. Also, while the lower-middle hero may occasionally have doubts about the social usefulness of his activities, and about the validity of his identity, the low culture hero does not. He is depicted as an explicitly classless person who expresses important working-class behavioral norms; he is sure of his masculinity, is shy with "good" women and sexually aggressive with "bad" ones. He works either alone or with "buddies" of the same sex, depends partly on luck and fate for success, and is distrustful of government and all institutionalized authority. Clark Gable, Gary Cooper, and John Wayne were typical prototypes of this hero, and the fact that none of the younger stars of today's action films have achieved their level of popularity is indicative of low culture's loss of dominance. Conversely, the confession magazine features the working-class girl's conflict between being sexually responsive in order to be popular with men, and remaining virginal until marriage. Family drama that deals sympathetically with the problems of both sexes at once has been rare.

In low culture, the performer is not only paramount but is often enjoyed as a "star," and vicarious contact is sought with him or her, for example, through the fan magazines that are read by younger members of the lower-culture public. Moreover, this public does not distinguish between performers and the characters they play; it likes its stars to play "themselves," that is, their public images. Writers and other creators receive little attention.

Low culture is provided through the mass media, but despite the size of this public, it must share much of its content with lower-middle culture. Often it does so by reinterpreting lower-middle-class content to fit working-class values. For example, in a working-class population that I studied, people watching a detective serial questioned the integrity of the policeman-hero and identified instead with the working-class characters who helped him catch the criminal. They also protested or made fun of the lower-middle-class heroes and values they saw depicted in other programs and commercials.[17]

Exclusively, low culture content exists as well, but since this public lacks the purchasing power to attract major national advertisers, its media can survive economically only by producing content of low technical quality for a very large audience. Moreover, partly because of poor schooling, low culture publics do not read much. As a result, they are served by a handful of tabloid dailies and weeklies, some with the highest newsstand sales among newspapers, which report sensational and violent activities—or invented activities—by celebrities and ordinary people.

Most Hollywood films were once made for the low culture public, until it gravitated to television. Although it shares this medium with lower-middle culture publics, initially network programming catered extensively to low culture, for example, by providing Westerns, the comic action of Lucille Ball and Red Skelton, the acrobatic vaudeville of the Ed Sullivan Show, and situation comedies like "Beverly Hillbillies" (which described how working-class people of rural origin outwit the more sophisticated and powerful urban middle class), and the music of Lawrence Welk. Some of these programs are disappearing from the network schedule as the low culture public shrinks in size and purchasing power, but the reruns survive on independent television stations, which are now perhaps the prime transmitters for low culture. This public is also served by independent radio stations which feature rock and country music and brief newscasts that use sound effects to imitate the attention-getting headline of the tabloid newspaper.

Low culture art reflects the sexual segregation of its public. The men often choose pinup pictures (of more overtly erotic and sexually aggressive-looking women than those featured in the upper-middle culture *Playboy*), which they hang in factories and garage workshops. The women like religious art and secular representational pictures with vivid colors. Home furnishings reflect the same aesthetic: they must be solid looking and "colorful." While high- and upper-middle-culture publics value starkness and simplicity, low-culture publics prefer ornateness—either in traditional, almost rococo, forms, or in the lavish contemporary style once described as "Hollywood modern."

QUASI-FOLK LOW CULTURE

This taste culture is a blend of folk culture and of the commercial low culture of the pre-World War II era, which catered to audiences who were just emerging from ethnic or rural folk cultures at the time. This is the taste culture of many poor people, who work in unskilled blue collar and service jobs and whose education ended in grade school; many of them rural or of rural origin and nonwhite. Although this public is still numerous, its low status and low purchasing power mean that its cultural needs receive little attention; by and large it must get along with low culture content.

Data about quasi-folk culture are scarce, but it seems to be a simpler version of low culture, with the same sexual segregation and emphasis on melodrama, action comedies, and morality plays in its content. This public's reading matter is tabloids and comic books; its films are old Westerns and adventure stories now shown only in sidestreet movie houses in the slums, and for Spanish-speaking audiences, the simple action films and soap operas made in Mexico. Partly because this culture is almost entirely ignored by the mass media, its public probably has retained more elements of folk culture than any other, which is recreated—and probably modernized—at church and street festivals and other social gatherings. Its younger people have recently taken to decorating public buildings and vehicles with elaborately painted and colorful graffiti, for example, in New York and Philadelphia. These graffiti usually consist of the names and street numbers of their artists, and may express their protest over being ignored by the rest of American society.

"Youth," Black, and Ethnic Cultures

My brief survey of taste publics and cultures has left out such recent developments as the so-called youth culture, the emergence of nationalistic cultures among blacks, Puerto Ricans, and other deprived minorities, and the revival of ethnic cultures among descendants of the European immigrants. This omission has been intentional, for these cultures may only be temporary offshoots from the taste cultures described previously.

"YOUTH" CULTURE

The last half of the 1960s saw the emergence of seemingly new cultures among young people, which were promptly collapsed under the label youth culture by adults. Even so, these cultures are neither entirely novel, nor limited to young people, nor so homogeneous as to be described by one label.

No culture is ever entirely new, and much of what is considered new resembles the bohemian culture that emerged after World War I, and the beat and hip cultures of the 1950s and the early 1960s. For example, the informality of dress and manners, the rejection of traditional forms of art and other high culture as in Dada, the use of drugs, the borrowing from black and folk cultures and the radical values can all be traced back to earlier avant-garde high culture. What is new, however, is the expansion of these high culture forms into the lower taste cultures, and the size of the public and the wide array of cultural fare it supports. These include new kinds of rock and folk music, movies, and newspapers, psychedelic and multimedia art, new fashions from tie-dyed to unisex clothing, as well as posters and the paraphernalia of the drug culture. The new cultural products are complemented by other kinds of cultural innovation which go beyond taste culture, for example, new forms of familial and communal living.

Although these innovations are often described by the mass media as parts of a single culture, they are actually traceable to several different ones. Moreover, these cultures exist at two levels: as *total* cultures which seek to exist apart from mainstream or straight society and in fact to change or overthrow it; and as *partial* cultures which, like the taste cultures described previously, are practiced by people who still "belong" to mainstream society.

Among the total cultures, at least five can be identified. The first is the original hippie culture which seems by now to have become a *drug-and-music* culture, insofar as its standards, products, and ways of living revolve around the use of drugs and "acid rock." The second is a *communal* culture, which is inventing new styles of familial, community, and economic life, often in communes, some seeking to recreate pastoral societies, tribal life, and the extended family. The third is a *political* culture which, though split into many factions, seeks to replace American capitalism with one or another form of radical socialism or anarchism through revolutionary though not necessarily violent means. These cultures are by no means mutually exclusive; rather, each places major emphasis on one theme, but some people participate in two or all three. However, participants in the drug culture appear to be more hedonistic and mystical than the rest; those in the communal culture are more concerned with social invention; and those in the political culture are dedicated to revolution, opposing drug use, mysticism, and sexual innovation as counterrevolutionary. The fourth culture is perhaps best labeled *neo-dadaist*. Typified by the "Yippies," it is an amalgam of the previous three but emphasizes the creation of new social, cultural, and political forms less as an end in itself than as a method of criticizing the equivalent institutions of mainstream society.[18] The fifth culture is a *religious* one, typified by the "Jesus freaks" and the Hare Krishna cult, which is a traditionalist reaction to the other four, preaching adherence to the absolutist moral codes of a theocratic community, and often to an asexual, apolitical, and drugless way of life.

The number of participants in these total cultures is small, probably less than 100,000 the country over, but their activities are highly visible because they are extensively covered by the mass media. Moreover, the total cultures are far more important than the number of participants would suggest, because they serve as models for the partial cultures, the participants in which number in the millions. Most of the people immersed in the total cultures are young people without familial responsibilities, many of whom are likely to drop out or transfer to a partial culture when they begin to raise their own families. The communal culture is much more familistic, however, although many of its participants seem to be single, and may move from commune to commune in their search for a life style that fits their needs. Since these total cultures, and particularly the drug and political ones face considerable hostility from mainstream society, only time will tell whether they can continue to grow or even to survive, other than as sources of inspiration for partial cultures.

The partial cultures are part-time versions of the total cultures, supported by people who maintain their economic position and social status in mainstream society, participating in them only on evenings and weekends. Whereas the fulltime participants in the total cultures are creator-oriented, viewing themselves as artists whose art is concerned with creating an entirely new American culture, the part-timers are user-oriented. Because they are far more numerous than the participants of the total culture, they become profitable audiences for commercial distributors for partial culture products, particularly music, posters, and clothing. In fact, some of the partial cultures are in the process of becoming the newest avant-garde factions of various mainstream taste cultures, not only because their products are created commercially but because these products are altered as they are borrowed from the total culture, becoming more similar to mainstream cultural products in the process. For example, the most popular posters are much closer in style to progressive upper or lower-middle art than to the neo-Art Nouveau or pseudo-Indian styles originally developed by the hippies.

Although the partial cultures are derived from the total ones, they are also differentiated on the basis of class, reflecting to some extent the standards of the mainstream taste cultures for which they serve as radical avant-gardes. Roszak's counterculture is, in purpose, method, style, and subtlety, far closer to mainstream high culture than, for example, to the drug-and-music culture of working-class youths, even though they share some values. Similarly, the various upper-middle partial cultures, which find expression in such journals as the *Village Voice* or *Rolling Stone*, are quite different from the lower-middle partial cultures, the products of which are to be found in New York's Greenwich Village and Los Angeles' Sunset Strip. The taste differences between the two publics have not yet been studied, but while both currently gravitate to rock music, I suspect that the young people of the upper-middle public are more likely to choose esoteric and experimental forms of rock and the politically oriented folk rock; and lower-middle and low publics, the more conventional rock forms and lyrics that deal with the trials and tribulations of love. Similarly, I would expect Bob Dylan to be more popular with "higher" taste publics; an action-oriented "belter" like the late Janis Joplin, with "lower" publics.

Other differences between the various cultures can also be identified. For example, Roszak's counterculture is emphatically antitechnological, while most others not only favor the peaceful uses of technology but employ the latest inventions in musical, film, and vehicular technology. Some communes reject mass-produced goods and make their own clothing and furniture; others use commercial products and experiment with the latest architectural technology.

Still, the total and partial cultures I have described also share many values. They are all opposed to various aspects of mainstream society, particularly its proclivity to war, the economic and generational inequality of the domestic society, and the hypocrisy resulting from the sizable gap between announced societal values and public policies. All these cultures also rely on drugs more than liquor; they emphasize community over individual concerns—even if some also stress "doing your own thing"; they give higher priority to the expression of feelings than the application of reason; they prefer film, music, and art to the print culture and they reject the sexual norms of mainstream society—although these norms are no longer sacrosanct among the younger people who remain in it. Finally, they all reflect and react to the interstitial and ambiguous position which adolescents and young adults are forced to occupy in a society which still often treats them like children, particularly when they are not in the mainstream labor force.

For that reason, it is possible to label all the cultures I have described as kinds of youth culture, although their rejection of mainstream society has less to do with the generation gap than with a fundamental difference of values that is neither limited to the young alone, nor shared by all young people. Actually, the value difference is much more a function of class, for the young cultural and political radicals come primarily from the professional upper-middle classes, and the values they reject are those of the managerial upper and upper-middle classes, and of their supporters in the lower-middle and working classes.[19] They are fighting the present economic system: the capitalists and corporate managers who run it, and the white and blue collar workers who support it partly because they depend on it for their livelihood. They are also struggling against the bureaucratization of society, both in private enterprise and the public agencies, and especially against the bureaucratization of intellectual and professional work, which threatens to reduce the control of intellectuals and professionals over their work.

Thus, the young radicals are fighting much the same groups as the socialist critics of mass culture, who also oppose the business-dominated society. At the same time, however, they are not advocating the same values; the young radicals are seeking to create an entirely different society, and are not particularly interested in protecting high culture. Indeed, the radicals and critics are enemies, some of the critics having attacked the radicals as romantic revolutionaries—and even left-wing fascists—while the radicals condemn the critics as defenders of the status quo.[20] Much of the conflict between the two groups has centered on the university; the radicals rejecting it for its dependence on and support of the corporate economy; the critics seeking to preserve it because it has become the major repository and financial support of high culture.

In the historical long run, however, both radicals and mass culture critics may turn out to fall into the same category; both have been defending some victims of the evolution of urban-industrial society, although they defend different victims and different ideals. The critics are, as I suggested in Chapter One, speaking for a high culture which has lost its cultural dominance with the development and growth of commercial popular cultures, while many of the radicals are fighting a rearguard action against the bureaucratization of upper-middle class occupations. Although some are groping for the development of a new culture based less on the scarcity of money and more on the scarcity of work, that is, a culture which will be needed when people no longer put in forty-hour workweeks, others, particularly those who place major stress on "doing your own thing" or going into carpentry and other forms of individual craftsmanship, are rebels against the emergence of intellectual and professional assembly lines.

In part, the conflict between the radicals and the critics is over the importance of the democratic ideal; the radicals want to create a new culture even if their methods of doing so are sometimes undemocratic—and the critics stress this failing in their attack. Conversely, the critics want to preserve high culture, and will support the mainstream economic and political institutions for this purpose, even if some of the methods of these institutions are undemocratic—and the radicals attack the critics for their blindness to these methods.

BLACK CULTURE

Although a conscious and deliberately created black culture emerged into visibility—at least to whites—only in the last half of the 1960s, it, like the Puerto Rican, Chicano, and Chinese cultures now developing among similarly deprived racial and quasi-racial groups, is by no means new. Black cultural content of all kinds has existed ever since blacks were brought to America, and black music has been borrowed by whites regularly for over a century.[21] What is new about black culture is a recent increase in vitality, which accounts for its greater visibility to whites. The new vitality results partly from the growth of the educated black middle class and the relaxation of segregationist barriers, but also from the need for culture of the civil rights and black power movements. In fact, the newer elements of black culture—and its Puerto Rican, Chicano, or other equivalents—can be described as nationalistic, existing partly to improve the political position of the black community in America. Most of the content of new black culture is directly or indirectly political, expressing, demanding, and justifying the legitimacy of a black identity and a black tradition in order to establish a cultural basis for racial equality.

Despite its recent growth, black culture remains a partial culture, for in many aspects of living, blacks share the taste cultures created by whites, and their aesthetic standards, leisure, and consumption habits are little different from whites of similar socioeconomic level and age. Although they listen to black radio stations, read black newspapers and magazines, and watch the few genuinely black films and television programs, they also use the media created predominantly by and for whites, and according to at least one study, they use it more than whites.[22] Most of them also seem to enjoy the content of the predominantly white media, although such a generalization cannot properly be made until they have an opportunity to choose between black and white content. Some preference studies have shown, however, that when blacks are asked to choose between hypothetical all-black and all-white entertainment, a majority will choose the former, but when they can also choose integrated entertainment, almost all prefer it to both black and white programming.[23]

ETHNIC CULTURES

The European immigrants brought their own taste cultures with them to America, but because most of the immigrants, except for some Jews, were uneducated peasants and landless laborers who spent most of their waking hours at work, their taste cultures were sparse, and dominated by compensatory content to cope with and escape from deprivation. As a result, these taste cultures emphasized family life, eating or drinking, and religion. The cultures were maintained by the immigrants, partly for language reasons, but they were quickly eroded by acculturation in the second generation, not being rich enough in content to fill the increased leisure time available to this generation, and being too religious to satisfy its more secular leisure preferences. In addition, the immigrant taste cultures were mainly folk and quasi-folk low cultures. When the immigrants or their children became upwardly mobile and wanted taste culture of greater sophistication and higher status, they found it easier to choose from American cultures than to upgrade the immigrant low culture or to import higher status cultures from their country of origin. Some Jewish taste culture was Americanized, but the peasant taste cultures, for example, Polish, Italian, Greek, have virtually disappeared except for traditional foods and religious practices—and a few dances and songs which are performed at occasional ethnic festivals.

Some observers have reported a revival of ethnic cultures among Italians, Poles, and other third- and fourth-generation descendants of the European immigrants.[24] There is as yet no reliable empirical evidence of such a revival, however, other than among a handful of ethnic intellectuals. In fact, the latest community studies among American ethnic groups suggest, as did earlier ones, that by the third or fourth generation, acculturation is almost complete.[25] Although assimilation has proceeded much more slowly, so that ethnic familial and other social structures continue to persist, most contemporary "ethnics" live like other Americans of similar age and socioeconomic status, indulging in the panethnic food culture of pizza, cornbeef, and shish kebab that the supermarket has made available to everyone.

What has been revived or at least made more visible, however, is ethnic politics, mainly as a reaction by urban white working-class people to increased black political activity. Phenomena like the ethnically balanced political ticket have never succumbed to acculturation; but since the late 1960s, sporadic upsurges of ethnic pride have emerged, for example, protest by Italians against the identification of organized crime with the Mafia, and by Poles against "Polish jokes." Even so, most ethnic political activity has been panethnic, that is, working-class politicians of ethnic background have been supported by working-class voters from all ethnic groups, rather than by just their ethnic peers as in the past, particularly when running against blacks or white upper-middle-class reformers. In these instances, however, ethnicity is only a euphemistic cover for class. For example, when Mario Procaccino ran against John Lindsay in the 1968 New York mayoralty election, he campaigned not as an Italian, but as the candidate of the "little people" against the "limousine liberals." Whatever feelings of ethnic pride and identity develop during these election campaigns disappear afterward, however, and there is no indication that they have led to a revival of individual ethnic cultures.

The Social Structure of Taste Publics and Cultures

The analysis of individual taste publics and cultures has underplayed the extent to which they are related to each other and to the larger society. In reality, taste publics and cultures are not only independent aggregates, but must also be viewed as parts of an overall *taste structure*, by which I mean the sum of the relationships that take place between different publics and cultures. The taste structure is in turn part of the larger social structure.

TASTE, SOCIAL STRUCTURE, AND POLITICS

One of the more important relationships between taste culture and the larger society is political. Although most taste cultures are not explicitly political, all cultural content expresses values that can become political or have political consequences. Even the simplest television family comedy,

103

for example, says something about the relations between men and women and parents and children, and insofar as these relations involve values and questions of power they are political, although they may not be recognized as such until the relations are questioned. Consequently, the use of women as sexual objects in advertising only became a political issue with the emergence of women's liberation.

As noted earlier, the mass culture critique is in part political, advocating both conservative and socialist policies, but one of the major contributions of the new radical and black cultures has been to identify the implicit political assumptions of all mainstream taste cultures, high and low, and to argue that all culture has political implications. The socialist critics of mass culture had already pointed to conservative political values in popular culture, but these critics did not often dwell on similar values in high culture. As a result both socialist and conservative defenders of high culture were disturbed when radicals and militant blacks identified conservative values in high culture. Equally important, the radicals argued that culture could not remain "above" politics, which some defenders of high culture have deplored as the politicization of culture. Politicization serves to make the political values in high culture (and popular culture) visible, forces discussion of these values, and leads to criticism of culture as conservative or radical.

The political values of the various taste cultures are difficult to identify with any degree of accuracy, because, as noted earlier, the products associated with these cultures are more visible than the values of the people choosing them, and it is risky to infer people's values from the products. For example, although low culture products are often conservative, opinion polls among working-class and poor people, who make up the low culture public, indicate that many are by no means conservative, particularly around economic issues. Rather, they lack cultural products to express their values.

The political values expressed in the various taste cultures range from Far Right to Far Left, although media products shun the extremes. High culture may include these extremes more often than other cultures, but Far Right values are to be found mainly among the classics, the dominance of liberal opinion among the high culture public having placed right-wing high culture in disrepute.[26] Upper-middle culture products are liberal, conservative, or centrist, and the remaining taste culture products are mainly centrist or conservative. In part, their conservatism reflects the business ideology of the mass media's owners and managers, but often the business-man's desire not to antagonize the vocal, even if not sizable, number of conservatives in the audience is more important. Frequently, small conservative pressure groups are able to raise a sufficient public outcry to force changes in media policy, for example, to ban a politically controversial televi-sion program, although they are usually successful only in influencing local stations (or newspapers). The national news and entertainment media are not immune to conservative (or liberal) pressure, but they are far less likely to give in to pressure, although they may review their policies and prac-tices afterward.

Actually, however, media conservatism is more often cultural than political, and most censorship or self-censorship by media creators is aimed at excising profanity and sexual or sacrilegious references that might antagonize what media people call "the hinterland." This is probably the major reason for the obvious slowness of television to liberalize its content dealing with sexual norms and behavior patterns.

Black performers and black content began to appear in entertainment fare after the ghetto upheavals finally forced media executives to pay attention to civil rights groups, which had long demanded more employment of black per-formers. By the 1970s, prime-time television even featured several comedy series about blacks, for example, "Sanford and Son," and "Good Times," which are made to appeal to white as well as black viewers. Although both series center their humor mainly around a class issue, whether their leading characters should abide by the norms of middle-class respectability, they also question white stereotypes of blacks and include pointed if not very militant black criticism of white behavior vis-á-vis blacks and of white-dominated institutions. This pattern was actually initiated by Leroy, Archie Bunker's young black neighbor in "All in the Family," who is, incidentally, one of the few characters in this popular program who is always presented as intelligent, and whose critical observations about racial issues are not subject to humorous rebuttal. Similarly, television, like other lower-middle media, has incorporated other topical issues, such as ecology and women's liberation, into popular dramas and comedies, although this may be less a response to audience interest than to the preoccupations of media creators who are either personally concerned about such issues or are searching for new story ideas.

The political implications of high and popular culture content are more difficult to describe. As noted earlier, the effects studies suggest that the media have only limited impact on political attitudes and behavior, but since politicians use news media content as one index of how their constituencies feel, newspaper and television editorials probably have more political impact than justified by reader interest. Moreover, the news media play an important political role by giving exposure and publicity to the people and activities they report on, and are thought to provide legitimization and status to them as well. Although their actual political impact on the audience is far smaller than the perceived impact, it is the latter to which politicians pay attention.

Journalists tend to be more liberal than their audiences, and although they try to report in an objective and detached manner, liberal values affect the selection of stories and their coverage. The national news media try to "play it down the middle" in order not to antagonize the supposedly centrist majority of the audience, even though they often report on radical activity because it has dramatic news value. They do not accurately reflect the social pluralism that exists in America, however; they see the world from a middle-class, middle-aged perspective, and thus give short shrift to the views of the young, the black, the poor, and even the working and lower-middle classes. Local news media tend to be even more conservative. Although high and upper-middle culture support several "journals of opinion" to express diverse points of view, the lower taste cultures are not as well supplied. Since the poor cannot afford to own—or even buy—magazines, their views and demands receive little public exposure.[27]

Criticism of the political values implicit in the media has come mainly from the Right and the Left, partly because they resent the antagonistic tone that slips into even objective reporting, partly because both think that if the media reported their views and activities in more detail, they could win more of the audience to their respective sides. Like all other political groups, they feel that the news media exist to portray and promote their own views, but since the news media provide more access to the political ins than the outs, and to the major political organizations than the minor ones, their criticism deserves attention.

The apolitical quality of most mass media fare other than news might suggest that treating popular culture as political is inaccurate or at best irrelevant. Conversely, from a revolutionary perspective such as Marcuse's, all taste culture is political, for even if it eschews politics, its failure to advance the revolutionary cause makes it politically reactionary; in Eldridge Cleaver's words, if it is not part of the solution, it is part of the problem. Yet even from a nonrevolutionary perspective, taste culture is ultimately political, insofar as it depicts one view of society to the exclusion of others, or reinforces one set of values and attitudes rather than another. Most people, whether as members of taste publics or as citizens, pay only a limited amount of attention to politics, however, which is why most taste cultures provide little explicitly political content. Consequently, while it is correct to argue that all culture is political, that argument is politically relevant only for people for whom politics is of major importance, for the rest of the population is not likely to care—or even notice—the political values which are implicit in their taste cultures. When such values are dominant in a society, they are generally assumed to be nonpolitical and even the repeated unmasking of these values, particularly by powerless groups, will not bring about much content change. For example, while black protest—together with the increased affluence of parts of the black population—has resulted in the creation of films with black heroes and characters since the late 1960s, it has not yet changed the content of most of these films, which still reflects much the same values as "white" films of similar genre.[28]

THE TASTE STRUCTURE

All of the taste cultures and publics coexist within what might be called a taste structure, which establishes and facilitates relationships between cultures and publics. Such relationships, which may be both peaceful and conflict-ridden, exist because some publics choose from more than one culture, and one taste culture may have to serve a number of publics. The most important reason for the existence of a taste structure, however, is the nature of the larger society, particularly its socioeconomic hierarchy. All taste publics and cultures participate in and are affected by this hierarchy and the taste structure itself is hierarchical.

Although most people probably restrict their content

choices to one culture or to two "adjacent" ones, everyone occasionally chooses from a much higher or lower culture. Such "cultural straddling" can be both downward and upward; it is the former when members of the high culture public choose detective stories for their light reading or watch football games on Sunday after having visited art galleries on Saturday, or when they and members of middle culture publics go to a burlesque theater. Straddling is upward, for example, when members of the lower-middle and low culture publics make an annual or semi-annual visit to a museum that exhibits primarily high culture art. Upward straddling sometimes involves explicit status motivations, as when people choose from a "higher" culture for "status-seeking" purposes or to encourage cultural mobility on the part of their children; downward straddling is usually justified by the need for catharsis or relief from the cultural routine. Even so, downward straddling, at least among high culture publics, is limited by the low status of the other cultures and is informally regulated so as to make only a small number of their products eligible for straddling. From time to time, higher culture publics—and publications—try to suggest which of these products are "in" and "out," or as Nancy Mitford once put it, "U" and "non-U."[29] Because status considerations are important, higher culture publics frequently take up popular culture only after it has been dropped by its original users; during the 1960s and 1970s, for instance, the films of Humphrey Bogart and the Hollywood musicals of Busby Berkeley were popular with higher culture publics.

As already noted, people who are creator-oriented in one field of high culture may be user-oriented in another, and may even prefer middle-culture choices outside their area of creator-oriented specialization. Susan Sontag has pointed out that "one of the facts to be reckoned with is that taste tends to develop unevenly. It's rare that the same person has good [i.e., creator-oriented high culture] visual taste and good taste in people and good taste in ideas."[30] The mixture of creator- and user-orientation exists in all taste publics, however, and persons from lower-middle culture who paint may have good taste in art, by Sontag's terminology, but not in other cultural choices.

In addition, there is mobility of choice, for some people are upwardly mobile culturally as well as socially. Usually, this mobility occurs during the school years, with college a major cause of the move to a higher taste culture. Mobility often ceases with parenthood, when the amount and complexity of reading, and going out to the theater or the movies decreases. In old age, further downward mobility may occur as the content people found gratifying in their youth becomes too difficult or upsetting.

Content also moves between cultures. Thus, a book written for a high-culture public may be made available to the upper-middle one through an article in *Harper's*, which is then cut and edited to appear in the *Reader's Digest*. Eventually, the central thesis of the book might even receive passing mention in a low culture publication. As cultures borrow from one another, content is often transformed to make it understandable or acceptable to different publics, and it is this aspect of borrowing which the mass culture critics resent the most.

Occasionally, a specific cultural product or a performer may appeal to several publics at once and thus become extraordinarily successful, for example, the comic strips "Peanuts" and "Pogo," or performers such as Charlie Chaplin and Marilyn Monroe. Generally speaking, the multicultural appeal is possible because the content is such as to enable every public to see something in it to meet its wants. Thus Charlie Chaplin was seen as a slapstick comic and clown by the lower cultures, and a satirical critic of society by higher ones. Once in a while, a product is accepted by all cultures because it conforms to aesthetic standards that are shared by all of them, but this is rare because there is so little agreement about what is beautiful or entertaining.

Finally, and in some ways most important, content is shared because several of the taste cultures are served by the same medium. For example, commercial television must serve all cultures, although in practice it serves primarily lower-middle and lower culture publics, offering higher culture content mainly to meet the public service requirements of the Federal Communications Commission. Much of the effort and anxiety of television programming executives stem from their attempt to find content that will be acceptable to the major taste publics and their various age groups. When Hollywood makes high budget films, it plans for content that will appeal to as many publics as possible, for example, by including characters which can be played by stars who appeal to diverse age groups.

Since most cultural content is distributed commercially, the taste structure is guided by much the same rules as the rest of the economy, the creators and the firms that hire them selling their products to those customers who can afford them, and ignoring those who cannot. The sellers try to secure their markets and limit competition destructive to them; the buyers seek to exert some control over the sellers through their buying decisions. It is also possible to view these relationships in political terms, with the creators, like politicians, offering alternatives, and audiences, like voters, choosing among them, or complaining about the lack of viable choices, like radicals. Television networks compete with each other like political parties as well as businesses, and the careers of network executives, as of politicians, ride on their ability to guess what the audience will accept. They are aided by the fact that taste, like party preference, is related to socioeconomic background and is therefore relatively stable; more stable, in fact, than political "taste," and popular television and movie stars remain "in office" longer than popular politicians. For example, Ed Sullivan and Bob Hope outlasted even many senators from one-party states. The media's need to appeal to several taste publics at once forces them to act like political parties whose constituencies cut across class lines and include opposing interest groups.

The publics themselves can be conceived as interest groups, for they are competing with others to make sure that the content they want is created. When resources are scarce, as with television channels, or when values are contradictory, as with high culture's espousal of abstraction and low culture's hostility to it, there is likely to be conflict among publics. Since these do not exist as organized groups, however, and lack an arena in which they can fight, the conflict normally takes place between creators and distributors. As I indicated earlier, mass media creation is a group process and group members often function as self-appointed representatives of conflicting taste publics, competing among themselves to determine which public will be given first priority in the content.

A particularly interesting example of cultural conflict and cultural power struggle arises periodically over the regulation of pornography. For a variety of reasons, some of them having to do with the cultural characteristics of its major users, at least in the past, pornography—especially of the hard-core variety—has observed the norms of low culture, and since very little middle or high culture pornography is created, pornography users from these publics must suffer the esthetic tortures of its low culture trappings. Since the most vocal opponents of pornography are, however, also against the use of erotic content in otherwise non-pornographic films and novels, the resulting legislation often condemns both low culture pornography and high and upper-middle culture products with some erotic content. At this point, defenders of upper-middle and high culture publics join with civil liberties organizations to protect their own culture, and to exempt such works as *Ulysses* and *Studs Lonigan*, and, more recently, the film *Carnal Knowledge* from antipornography legislation. The Supreme Court's ruling that content which has "some redeeming social value" should not be censored as pornographic has in the past protected high and upper-middle culture with erotic themes, but in 1973, the Supreme Court transferred the censorship power to local communities. In areas where sexual conservatives are politically powerful and the defenders of upper-middle and high culture weak, antipornography rulings may be used to censor these two cultures, with erotic content sometimes only serving as an excuse to keep out content which threatens the holders of cultural and political power for other reasons and on other, nonsexual, grounds.

As in the political arena, some participants have more power than others, and some are excluded altogether, for example, the poor, the old, and others with little purchasing power. Creators have more power than consumers, since the latter can only veto what the former offer, although audience protest can affect media content. And like all structures that deal with profits and power, the taste structure is hierarchical. Today, economic dominance is located in the mass media—and their corporate sponsors—which cater to the lower-middle public, since it is the largest and has the most purchasing power. This dominance is accompanied by some political power, as may be seen by the reluctance of the Federal Communications Commission to enforce the Commission requirements for public service programming, this being of interest primarily to upper-middle publics. Upper-middle culture has some power over public allocations for culture, because the civic leaders who stand behind public television or local cultural complexes like New York's Lincoln Center are usually businessmen from the upper-middle public. Much to the chagrin of high culture, they tend to prefer upper-middle culture to high culture, and within the latter, establishment to avant-garde content. Radicals reject the hierarchy altogether, but are powerless to stop the borrowing and transformation of their cultural products.

THE TASTE HIERARCHY

The taste hierarchy differs somewhat from the larger class hierarchy of which it is a part. In the American class hierarchy, the upper and upper-middle classes are more powerful than the lower-middle and working classes of Middle America, although when Middle Americans are interested in a specific political issue, they can often get their way. In the taste hierarchy, Middle America has much more power, at least indirect power, because the lower-middle public is the audience to which the mass media must appeal. Conflict exists in the taste hierarchy as in the class hierarchy, but conflict between taste publics differs from class conflict in part because taste interests result in the organization of politically active interest groups even less often than class interests, in part because cultural issues are usually not as important to people as class issues, and in part because the audience is not accustomed to exerting political pressure about cultural matters. Some viewers may contact their television station if their favorite program is threatened with cancellation, but they do not seem to get upset in large numbers about what is shown on television on a day-to-day basis, except to children.

More important, there seems to be less resentment about cultural inequality than about other kinds of inequality. While poorer people want the money and power available to upper income groups, lower taste publics apparently do not feel deprived by their inability to participate in higher taste cultures. They want the same amount of education, but for occupational and social mobility rather than cultural mobility, and when people obtain more income and status, they often remain in their original taste public. They may buy the housing, appliances, boats, and vacations, but not the art and music that go with higher income. Even educational mobility does not always bring about a striving for cultural mobility; for example, in their leisure behavior, many college professors belong to the lower-middle taste public. The absence of relative deprivation over cultural inequality makes the conflict between taste publics much milder than the conflict between income groups, and, for that matter, between religious groups.

While the taste hierarchy differs from the class hierarchy, it is quite similar to the status hierarchy, for in terms of prestige, high culture is at the top and low culture is at the bottom. Decisions about cultural choices often reflect status considerations, and when a culture of lower status borrows the content of a higher one, the latter usually drops the item from its cultural repertoire. As I suggested earlier, when Ingmar Bergman's films became popular with upper-middle moviegoers in the 1960s, they lost much of their standing among high culture film buffs. Even so, cultural prestige seems less important to most people than other kinds of prestige and upwardly mobile people will move quickly into a neighborhood that expresses their new status but may never adopt the taste culture associated with that status. This is particularly true of middle and lower status people, and reflects at least in part their lack of education which prevents cultural mobility. Nevertheless, even though the higher taste cultures have more prestige than the lower ones, people appear to be less interested in or anxious about cultural prestige than about other kinds.

The prestige of high culture derives from its historical alignment with the elite, its occasional alliance with High and Cafe Society in America, as well as from the status of its own public and its claim to cultural expertise, which is legitimated by the many creators, critics, and scholars in its public. Consequently, even though all taste publics claim their standards are best, high culture's claim receives more deference. Equally important, high culture standards are explicit and to some extent even codified; they are constantly applied in the literary journals, discussed by scholars and critics, and taught in the most prestigious universities. In fact, they are even taught in less prestigious colleges—where the English department is often a lonely bastion of high culture—and often as the only set of aesthetic standards in existence. The standards of the other taste cultures are rarely discussed and taught, and are thus implicit, uncodified, and for all practical purposes invisible. As a result, high culture has more influence than either the size or the status of its public would suggest.

This influence is felt in the mass media, too, because most of their creators are aware of the high culture standards even if they do not apply them. Film, theater, and television critics writing for newspapers and mass magazines are even more aware of them, although their criticism usually applies upper-middle standards despite the fact that much of their audience is lower-middle.[31] Moreover, they criticize mainly high and upper-middle content, regardless of the taste levels of their readers, so that, for example, the critics for the *New York Daily News*, with a principally low culture readership, sometimes review plays and foreign films that most of their readers never see.[32] Conversely, what most people see most often, the weekly installments of television series, receives no published criticism at all after the first installment. For this reason, lower taste publics become their own critics, disseminating their criticism in conversation with family members, friends, and fellow workers. This criticism is called "word of mouth" in the mass media and is more influential than that of the published critics in determining which popular novels, films, and television programs become "hits."[33] As a result, when successful popular culture creators are attacked by professional critics for their failure to meet high culture standards, these creators often reply that the only critic they respect is the audience, and if it buys their work, the judgment of the professional critics is either wrong or irrelevant.[34]

Nevertheless, the public dominance of high (and upper-middle) culture criticism encourages obeisance to the aesthetic standards of these two cultures, especially among people who place some value on being "cultured" or who are upwardly mobile. Such obeisance is also encouraged by status considerations; people in all cultures are loath to admit they use content popular among people of lower status than their own. Consequently, they often make distinctions between what they think publicly is good and what they choose privately. The advocates of high culture interpret the existence of this distinction as evidence of the universality of their own standards and conclude either that people want more high culture than they actually get, or that they prefer to choose what they think is bad rather than what they say is good. Both interpretations are inaccurate, however, and reflect the invisibility of the aesthetic standards of the other taste cultures.

The invisibility of the standards has other implications. For one thing, it hides the fact that these standards, like those of high culture, include criteria for bad content as well as good. Although some critics of mass culture have argued that only high culture can choose between good and bad content, the publics in other cultures make similar qualitative judgments. The people whose favorite type of drama is the Western can and do distinguish between good and bad ones in the same way as high culture theatergoers distinguish between good and bad plays. The theatergoers' judgment may be more sophisticated and more explicitly related to their standards, but this is only because their standards are explicit, because they have been trained in making judgments based on these standards, and because their judgments are supported by professional critics. The viewers of television Westerns lack the explicit standards and therefore the training to apply them, and they cannot resort to published criticism to test and sharpen their own views.

The difference between the two publics is in the amount of aesthetic training, but this does not justify assuming a difference in aesthetic concern. Thus low culture publics may think calendar art and overstuffed furniture as beautiful as upper culture publics consider abstract expressionist paintings and the latest in Italian furniture; the difference between them is in their ability to put their feelings into an aesthetic vocabulary. High culture housewives may have learned interior design in school or may be able to hire professional decorators, but every housewife of every taste culture who can afford to buy furniture seeks to make her rooms into a work of beauty expressing her standards. In this process she chooses form, color, and relationships between individual pieces, as does the trained decorator. The two housewives differ in the amount of training in their standards, the skill and resources available to put their standards into action, the verbal fluency with which they justify their choices, and, of course, in the content of their standards, in what they think is beautiful, but they are similar in that both are striving for beauty.[35]

CHAPTER THREE

The Evaluation of Taste Cultures and Publics

LIKE any other sociological analysis, my comparison of taste cultures has normative implications and can be developed into an evaluation by the addition of explicit value judgments.[1] Such an evaluation is not itself sociological, for value judgments cannot be justified empirically, although some of the consequences of such judgments can be tested.

Evaluations may be both private and public. The former is an individual's private choice for his own life; the latter deals with the welfare of society and is ultimately aimed at formulating public policy, and the two are not equivalent. For example, in their private lives, sociologists belong to a taste public like everyone else, and make their own cultural choices and private evaluations about the standards and content of other taste cultures accordingly, condemning those they dislike as too highbrow or lowbrow the same way as other people. If and when a sociologist takes on a public policy role, however, he or she cannot impose his or her private choices or evaluations on other people, but must take account of *their* private evaluations, and build them into public policy. Public policy need not be totally obeisant to them, but it cannot ignore them.

The critics of mass culture have, however, done precisely that; they have translated their own private evaluations into a public policy position which not only ignores other people's private evaluations but seeks to eliminate them altogether.

121

The critics demand that everyone should live by their standards and embrace high culture, but this demand is not justified in a democratic and pluralistic society, any more than the similar claims of other taste publics that their standards alone are desirable. The assumption of high culture's universality would be justified if the critics could prove that popular culture harmed society or a significant number of individuals, interfered with the achievement of the goals of the majority of citizens, or seriously endangered the goals of a minority. Since the critics have not provided such proof and since their standards are not shared by a majority of the population, it is necessary to develop a public evaluation that takes other standards into account.

Such an evaluation must begin by answering two questions: what is a good, or a socially desirable, taste culture; and what is a good, or a socially desirable, taste public. A desirable taste culture, I suggest, should satisfy at least the following criteria. First, it must respond to and express the demands of its users, offering cultural content that provides the aesthetic satisfaction, information, entertainment, and so forth, which they want or think is good. Second, a desirable taste culture must offer material and other rewards to creators; they must have the incentive to contribute to a culture, the feeling that their contribution meets their own needs as creators, and the knowledge that their users will want, or will at least accept, their creative work. Ideally, a desirable taste culture synthesizes the demands of both users and creators, and establishes a symbiotic relationship between them, doing so on an egalitarian basis wherever possible so that neither dominates the other. Third, a good taste culture must not be socially or psychologically harmful; it should not hurt its users, creators, or the rest of society.

Needless to say, these criteria are very simple, and raise many questions that would need to be answered in a more detailed analysis. For example, one could argue that a society which allocates most of its cultural funds to popular culture thereby harms high culture and its users, but public subsidies could be provided to high culture to a level at which such harm is eliminated.

In addition, yet other criteria could be added to my list. Thus, cultural vitality might be included as a criterion of desirability, but I would argue that even if this term could be defined operationally, vitality rests ultimately as much in the eye of the beholder as in a culture. Similarly, one might demand that a desirable culture enable its users to grow as individuals and as group members, but I am inclined to think that in a heterogeneous society, in which people can select from several cultures, they will choose cultural content which enables them to grow, and if they do not want to grow, no culture will persuade them to do so in any case. A desirable culture might also be socially relevant, or contribute to the public interest, but such a criterion makes culture into more of a political instrument than I suggested in Chapter One it could reasonably be expected to be, and besides, the mere attempt to decide what culture is or is not in the public interest raises the possibility of cultural dictatorship.

Criteria for the desirability of a taste public should not even be formulated. Although the mass culture critics argue that a taste public is desirable to the extent that it lives up to the standards of high culture, I would argue just the reverse: that high culture, and all taste cultures, must live up to the standards of their respective users and creators. Culture should not be harmful, but beyond that, it should serve its users and creators, and it should not become a Platonic ideal which must be served by its users and creators. If culture becomes an absolute good, as in the argument of the mass culture critics, then society is evaluated by the quality of its high culture, but such an evaluation strikes me as dangerous. For one thing, I believe the cultural level of a society is a less important criterion of a desirable society than some others, notably the extent to which a society provides a decent standard of living to all its members, without exploiting some for the benefit of others. Also, the historic comparison of societies on the basis of their cultural achievements, particularly in high culture, compares the activities of social elites without considering the costs which other members of the society may have paid for those activities. A public monument that requires the exploitation of the workers who build it may be beautiful—so beautiful that it becomes for many people the standard against which all other public buildings throughout the history are compared—but I would not consider it as an example of socially desirable culture.

Consequently, the evaluation to follow will compare taste cultures in terms of the wants and standards of their taste publics. This comparison also suffers from some oversimplification, for it assumes that taste cultures are homogeneous and that the same judgments can be made for all items within it. This assumption is unwarranted, however, for in any culture, some items will be desirable in terms of the three criteria I have proposed while others are not, and a proper evaluation would have to consider every cultural item in every taste culture, one by one. For example, it has recently been asserted that much avant-garde high culture music is overly formalistic and sterile, thus failing to respond to the demands of its users, and that contemporary popular music is far more vital and satisfying. This assertion can only be tested with the aid of empirical research among users, but while it may be accurate, it cannot be employed to condemn other items of high culture or praise other items of popular culture. However, my evaluation does not go into such detail, and is therefore a general statement which does not necessarily apply to any individual item within any taste culture.

Two Value Judgments about Taste Cultures and Publics

The evaluation begins with two value judgments, one about the taste cultures, the other about the taste publics.

If one compared the taste cultures alone, without taking into account the taste publics who choose them, it would be fair to say that the higher cultures are better or at least more comprehensive and more informative than the lower ones. This is my first value judgment. It is based on the assumption that the higher cultures may be better than the lower ones because they may be able to provide greater and perhaps more lasting aesthetic gratification, although this assumption still requires empirical testing among audiences from various publics.[2]

The higher cultures may also be more comprehensive; because their publics are better educated, these cultures can cover more spheres of life and encompass more ideas and symbols than the other cultures. For example, they can address themselves to philosophical issues in ways which are beyond the scope and expertise of the lower cultures. In addition, the higher cultures can borrow more widely from lower cultures, even if they rarely do so, whereas the lower cultures are restricted from extensive borrowing by the educational levels of their publics. Finally, the higher cultures may provide more adequate information to their users, helping them to comprehend their own social reality, to solve their personal and social problems, and to function as citizens better than other cultures do for their publics—although this assumption also requires empirical testing. Or to put it more simply, the higher cultures may be more functional for their users than the lower cultures are for theirs.

This value judgment bears some resemblance to the credo

125

of high culture advocates, but by itself, it is insufficient for public policy because, like the mass culture critique, it ignores the characteristics and wants of the people who choose culture. As stated, the judgment assumes that only culture is important, but that the users of culture are not important and, if it became the basis for public policy, it could be employed to impose culture on people against their will, much as totalitarian movements and regimes have tried to do.

In a democratic society, a policy-relevant value judgment must begin with the notion that taste cultures are chosen by people and cannot exist without them, so that the cultures cannot be evaluated without taking their publics into consideration. This requires a criterion by which cultures and publics can be evaluated jointly, and since every taste culture requires a certain amount of education from the taste public choosing it, amount of education is probably the best such criterion. People not only tend to choose the taste culture which is congruent with their education, but they cannot be expected to choose content which is incongruent with their education. Although elementary school graduates who have educated themselves to choose high culture deserve praise, their behavior is atypical, and to expect such behavior from everyone would be a demand for heroic behavior. Cultural heroism may be commendable, but any public policy which requires many people to act heroically is unenforceable, except perhaps in wartime, even if it is desirable.

The choice of high culture typically requires at least a high quality college education with strong emphasis on the humanities. Such a choice could therefore not be expected from a high school graduate, or for that matter from a college graduate untrained in the arts. For this reason the argument of mass culture critics that all college-educated people should choose high culture is not justified. Both the high school graduate and the college graduate should be expected to

126

choose content that fits their educational levels and aesthetic standards; and both should be judged negatively only if they consistently choose below these levels. A college graduate should not read mainly detective stories, nor should a high school graduate devote himself or herself to comic books. And while both deserve praise if they read Proust, they should not be expected to do so, at least not in evaluations that result in public policy.

I would argue, therefore, that if people seek aesthetic gratification and that if their cultural choices express their own values and taste standards, they are equally valid and desirable whether the culture is high or low. A person from a high culture public may choose abstract expressionist paintings while one from a low culture public selects calendar art, but both choose from content related to their standards and educational level. Moreover, both derive emotional and intellectual rewards from their choices, and both may add new ideas, feelings, and insights to their lives as a result. *The rewards may differ because their educational backgrounds and previous experiences differ, but the choices of both individuals result in additions to that experience.* The evaluation of people's choices cannot depend only on the content they choose but must compare what might be called the *incremental aesthetic reward* that results from their choices: the extent to which each person's choice adds something to his or her previous experience and his or her effort toward self-realization.[3] This incremental reward can be as great for a member of a low culture public as for a high culture one, for the reward has nothing to do with the quality of the cultural content; instead it judges the person's progress beyond his or her own past experience.[4]

My second value judgment argues, therefore, *that the evaluation of any taste culture must also take its taste public into account, that the evaluation of any item of cultural content must be related to the aesthetic standards and*

127

background characteristics of the relevant public, and that to the extent that all taste cultures reflect the characteristics and standards of their publics, they are equal in value. In other words, I do not believe that all taste cultures are of equal worth, but that they are of equal worth when considered in relation to their taste publics.

This judgment may seem to contradict the initial one, which argues the superiority of higher taste cultures, but the contradiction disappears if differences in taste publics are taken into consideration, and if the evaluation of taste cultures is accompanied by a recognition of the differential values and cultural skills of the various taste publics. The higher taste cultures may be more desirable when culture is abstracted and judged apart from its users, but the real world is not abstract, and the desirability of the higher cultures cannot be used as a guide to policy as long as lower taste publics lack the socioeconomic and educational opportunities prerequisite to choosing the higher cultures. The mass culture critics, especially the conservative ones, demand allegiance to high culture from people who lack the prerequisites they themselves possess; they ask for a society of high culture without at the same time concerning themselves with ways of enabling people to choose high culture.[5]

The two value judgments may now be combined into a policy judgment. *American society should pursue policies that would maximize educational and other opportunities for all so as to permit everyone to choose from higher taste cultures. Until such opportunities are available, however, it would be wrong to expect a society with a median educational level of twelve years to choose only from taste cultures requiring a college education, or for that matter, to support through public policies the welfare of the higher cultures at the expense of the lower ones. Moreover, it would be wrong to criticize people for holding and applying aesthetic standards that are related to their educational background, and for participating in taste cultures reflecting this background.*

This policy judgment might be called *aesthetic relationism*; it is a normative restatement of the concept of aesthetic pluralism used to describe the existence of diverse taste cultures.[6]

Two alternatives for public policy are implied by this statement. Either society must find ways of implementing the cultural mobility that would allow people to have the educational and socioeconomic background prerequisite to choice in the higher taste cultures; or, if these ways are not provided, it must permit the creation of cultural content which will meet the needs and standards of the existing taste publics.

Cultural Mobility

The policy of cultural mobility assumes that if every American had access to the income, education, and other background characteristics of the upper-middle class, many although not all would choose upper-middle or even high culture content. In all likelihood most people would choose the former, for high culture requires an extraordinary amount of emotional involvement with ideas and symbols that does not follow solely from being upper-middle class.[7] But even if everyone could participate in upper-middle taste culture, the overall taste level of American society would rise sharply, there would be a dramatic flowering of creativity within upper-middle culture, and there would most likely be more cultural diversity than at present. Of course, the lower taste cultures might decline and the variety they provide on the American scene would be reduced, but it is improper to argue for kinds of variety that require some people to be poor or poorly educated.

I would argue against a cultural mobility policy, however, and on several grounds. First, it is now patently impossible to raise all Americans to upper-middle-class income and educational levels; the former is financially impossible, the latter technically, given the scarcity of "good" schools and teachers. As a result, such a policy could only be implemented on a partial basis; only some people could be given upper-middle-class opportunities and probably only by reducing the opportunities of other people. Second, cultural mobility would require considerable redistribution of income and educational opportunity, but while I favor redistributive policies, they should be pursued for other goals: the elimination of poverty and other forms of economic inequality, as well as racial and political inequality.[8] In other words, egalitarian policies should be aimed at reducing the gap between the poor and the average American, rather than raising some people to upper-middle-class status to improve their taste. Even egalitarian economic policies would indirectly raise taste levels among some and at least increase opportunity for cultural choice among others, but the beneficiaries of such policies would not come up to upper-middle levels of taste, and insofar as greater equality for the poor would require some redistribution of income from the upper-middle class, it might reduce, if not levels of taste, then the funds for expressing them. Nevertheless, egalitarian economic policies have a far higher priority than cultural mobility.

This priority determination is based on two judgments, that a good life can be lived at all levels of taste, and that the overall taste level of a society is not as significant a criterion for the goodness of that society as the welfare of its members. To put the matter bluntly, neither high culture nor any other taste culture is at present so essential to society's welfare that it requires high priority for public programs for cultural mobility—at least not until there is evidence that lower (or higher) cultures hurt some people.[9]

This priority judgment applies especially to culture when it is an instrument of leisure; it cannot be applied so bluntly, however, when culture becomes a political instrument. If the choice of taste culture affected people's ability to function in the polity—or in the economy, for that matter—or if the creators of a given taste culture acted so as to consciously impair people in their ability to so function, then a quite different priority judgment would be necessary. As I noted in Chapter One, some radical and socialist critics of mass culture argue that popular culture impairs or at least diverts people from what they consider proper political behavior, and encourages "false consciousness," but, as I also suggested in that chapter, even the imposition of a revolutionary popular culture would not necessarily make people into revolutionaries.

I do not mean hereby to reject radical cultural change, or cultural reform, or cultural improvement per se, but to argue for concentrating on what appear to be the basic purposes of culture for most people: to achieve human self-realization and to enhance leisure time. Neither requires a high taste level. If people are able to strive for their own aesthetic standards and find cultural content that meets them, self-realization and a satisfying leisure life—that is, one marked by a minimum of boredom—are possible at all levels.

Moreover, as I noted earlier, rising incomes and the improvement of education are already producing a considerable amount of cultural mobility, and within less than a generation the dominant taste culture in America has moved from low to lower-middle. Although public policies for further cultural mobility may become more desirable in some future generation, if changes in the economy and technology reduce the length of the workday or workweek, the increase in leisure time expected in the next generation is not likely to exhaust existing leisure activity aspirations. Despite frequent expert pronouncements that most Americans cannot cope with more leisure time and that their resulting boredom could threaten the social order, most people now still lack sufficient leisure time, and sufficiently large blocks of such time to do all of the things they already want to do. Television viewing is as high as it is because most people have only a couple of hours between the time they put the children to bed and go to sleep themselves, and if they had more time, their evening hours would often be spent differently. If they had a greater number of long weekends and longer vacations, they would pursue many of the alternative indoor and outdoor activities that exist in every taste culture.[10]

The real threat to social order is not more leisure time, but feelings of social uselessness and anger brought about by unemployment, underemployment, and low incomes, and these feelings have nothing to do with leisure, for neither leisure per se nor the improved leisure education advocated by recreation experts can help people feel useful.[11] Feelings of social uselessness are most prevalent among the poor, and particularly among poor old and young people. Although the poor also suffer from inadequate leisure opportunites because they do not have enough money to buy the products of popular culture and because little cultural content is created for their needs, their prime requirements are good jobs, higher incomes, and better education. Once they obtain these, they can begin to think about their leisure time, but the same policies that would help them escape poverty would also remove many of the obstacles to self-realization and more gratifying leisure.

Cultural Pluralism and Subcultural Programming

In place of cultural mobility, I want to suggest a policy based on the concept of aesthetic relationism and the common sense notion of cultural pluralism: to provide cultural content to express and satisfy the specific standards of every taste public. I call this policy *subcultural programming*.

(Programming is an awkward term, but I use it instead of pluralism because the latter word has many different meanings these days and has become both a political catchword and a pejorative term. Programming is derived from radio and television, and many of the proposals to follow apply especially to television because it is today's most important mass medium, at least in terms of audience size, but I also mean the term to apply to content for other media, and to taste culture generally, however it is created. The prefix subcultural is chosen because, as I noted in the Introduction, taste cultures are actually subcultures.[12])

Instead of the present programming system, which provides content cutting across and thus compromising the standards of several taste publics and serving some not at all, subcultural programming would create for every taste public the specific taste culture which expresses its aesthetic standards. The taste publics I have in mind are narrower than those described previously, more sharply defined by class, age, and other factors, so that there might be specific programming for avant-grade low culture preadolescents, or for conventional upper-middle black young adults. The extent of subcultural specificity would be limited only by the actual existence of publics to be served, and by the financial and other costs of creating culture for a small audience.

Subcultural programming would enable audiences to find content best suited to their wants and needs, thus increasing their aesthetic and other satisfactions, and the relevance of their culture to their lives. In addition, it would considerably increase cultural diversity, enhancing and enriching American culture as a whole, high and low. It would also identify and then serve the taste publics which are served poorly today. Since it is unfortunately true that in American society those needing the most often get the least, currently the most poorly served groups are the low taste publics, the aged and the middle-aged in almost all taste publics, and more generally, all the people who are either low in purchasing power or who do not buy the kinds of products now advertised by the mass media.

For example, subcultural programming for poor people would be desirable, not only because present mass media programming ignores them and because its middle-class bias imposes further psychological stress on people who live amid an affluence they cannot share, but also because poor people are as entitled to their own culture as anyone else. Subcultural programming for the poor would differ from present media fare by focusing on topics of interest to this population, and by dealing with these topics from its own perspective. For example, in dramatic content, stories and characters would treat poor people as persons, not as misfits or unfortunate victims damaged by personal or economic difficulties. Although the poor are victimized by the American economy, media content about the poor, which seeks primarily to arouse the guilt or pity of more affluent audiences, can only be patronizing to the poor, who are exposed to it as well. Subcultural programming does not mean content which would encourage acquiescence with their living conditions—no content could produce that reaction in any case—but art, information, and entertainment that relate to their own experiences, interests, and problems, and through a culture which accepts their values and goals and speaks to their aesthetic standards and their language and art forms. And because "the poor" is a middle-class abstraction to describe a highly heterogeneous population, subcultural programming would have to be further specified for the different kinds and age groups of poor people.

Similarly, subcultural programming would mean more cultural content for the black, Puerto Rican and other racial and ethnic minority populations. Although the civil rights movement has persuaded the mass media to produce more content *about* blacks and to use more black performers, there is still too little television, radio, film, and even print *for* the diverse cultural needs of the majority of blacks. While it is doubtful that enough audience interest exists for the European ethnic cultures to justify ethnic cultural fare on a continuing basis, Americans from various ethnic groups, particularly those of working-class status, have interests and values which are not being catered to by the mass media, the popularity of the patronizing "All in the Family" notwithstanding. Subcultural programming would fill the cultural vacuum that now exists for Americanized working-class ethnics, and for other working-class people as well.

Even the high culture public could be included in the list of minorities poorly served by television and the other mass media, and subcultural programming can be useful to this public as well. Since high culture is already well supplied by non-mass media, however, its need for television programming may be of lower priority than that of other taste publics.

Finally, subcultural programming would alter the relationship between creators and consumers, for every creator would be able to work for and in a specific taste culture, rather than having to satisfy several at once. This would reduce alienation among creators, for in most instances, they could work for a taste public of their own choosing, one which shared their own standards. Creators would thus be able to create content that meets their needs while also involving the audience more intensively, emotionally as well as intellectually. Such programming would bring the creator closer to the audience, and under ideal conditions, would establish a modern form of the relationship said to have existed between folk artist and folk audience. Thus, it would also produce more creator-oriented popular culture.[13]

The Pros and Cons
of Subcultural Programming

I can best elaborate on the idea of subcultural programming by anticipating and meeting seven possible objections to it. *First,* subcultural programming might be interpreted as a policy of giving people inferior culture, rather than encouraging their use of high culture. This objection is justified, however, only if one accepts the assumptions of the mass culture critics that popular culture is inferior and that if it is not supplied people will eventually accept high culture. As I have tried to suggest, however, the educational and economic prerequisites of high culture use are such that it will always be the culture of a small public, thus retaining the exclusivity the critics of mass culture also want. Most people can and will choose the culture which coincides with their educational and class background, and deliberate policies to get them to choose other cultures are rarely effective. The previously noted failure of the Russian government to persuade its citizens to accept the official Communist culture and the inability of the British Broadcasting Corporation to convert English television viewers to high and upper-middle cultural fare during the ten years it had a monopoly over television programming suggest that governmental policy cannot easily alter audience preferences. Subcultural programming would accept the validity and legitimacy of these preferences, and would facilitate the growth and enrichment of the various taste cultures represented by these preferences.

Second, subcultural programming could be criticized as a policy to give people what they want, rather than what is good for them, and thus to justify current mass media practices. I do not believe, however, that giving people what other people think is good for them is desirable. This has always been the reformer's dream, even though few reformers can explain why what they think is good for people is better than what people think is good for them, particularly in the domains of culture, and often what reformers consider good for people also turns out to be good for the reformers, by providing them with more resources, jobs, or status. Still, I am not objecting to attempts at reform, as long as people have other choices and do not have to accept the reformer's fare involuntarily, and subcultural programming need not exclude cultural reform.

Moreover, subcultural programming is intended to give people *what they judge to be good rather than what they want,* and thus strives for the same level of excellence as high culture, except that the standards used to define excellence will differ among taste publics. The choice of good culture is not monopolized by the high culture public; most of the time, people from all taste publics want the art, information, and entertainment they judge to be good and, unless they are deliberately seeking escape, few will intentionally choose what they think is bad. Even so, one of the purposes of entertainment is to satisfy the wish for escape, among high culture publics as well as others, and I see nothing wrong with it, for everyone needs escape at some time. Perhaps the lower taste publics want more escape than the higher ones, but perhaps they also need more escape from the conditions in which they live, and to withhold cultural fare which satisfies that need without providing conditions which require less escape is punitive. Culture is not chosen in a vacuum, and to deprive people of escapist culture in the hope of reforming them is a spurious policy; it treats the effects of deprivation and not the cause. Escapist culture which harms the user and the society should not be provided if proof of its harmfulness can be established. Similarly, immoderate resort to cultural content which people think is bad is undesirable, but such resort is self-punishment rather than escape, and has more to do with social or individual pathology than with choice of culture.

Nevertheless, subcultural programming which gives people what they want is not equivalent to justifying current mass media practices. Although media decision makers sometimes defend their policies by arguing that they are giving people what they want, subcultural programming would have the media provide content people think is good. The media have not pursued such a policy and it is not clear that they even give their audiences what they want. For one thing, recent polls of television viewers suggest that there is dissatisfaction with a great deal of television fare, particularly entertainment, and that this dissatisfaction exists not just among the higher taste publics but among the very publics to which television is explicitly catering.[14] Moreover, the media cannot give their audiences what these audiences want or think is good, because what little feedback they now obtain from the audience is incomplete and poor. The programming decisions of network television are largely determined by the Nielsen ratings, drawn from a sample of about 1200 households. This method, which counts sets in use, not people watching, and supplements these data by a brief diary, is not only unable to measure viewer evaluations but does not provide a sample large enough to take account of the diversity of the total audience.[15] To be sure, a larger sample might not result in radically different ratings for current programs, but a rating system which included data on viewer evaluation would indicate the amount and intensity of satisfaction or dissatisfaction, and might even suggest where subcultural programming is most needed.

Other mass media feedback mechanisms are equally deficient. The movies use box office figures, but these only reflect a decision to see a film, not a reaction to or evaluation of films seen. Magazine readership studies do provide reactions to published content, but these studies are conducted by advertising departments and are rarely used for feedback to editorial policies, except when readership is declining precipitously. Actually, most mass media are not interested in providing content to meet either the wants or aesthetic standards of their audiences; they want to sell advertising and to persuade audiences to buy the advertised goods, and while they provide content which will attract audiences for the advertisers, this has little to do with satisfying the aesthetic standards of the audience. The media generally aim to provide advertisers with the largest audience at the lowest cost—the cost per thousand formula—which requires them to attract the largest possible audience for many items of media fare; subcultural programming, on the other hand, would create much more and more diverse fare, thus resulting in smaller audiences for each item of content.

Third, subcultural programming could be condemned for encouraging the creation of socially undesirable content, harmful to the achievement of universally shared goals or of the goals of individual users. This objection is valid only if one assumes that most people are socially destructive or self-destructive, an assumption I find unacceptable. Moreover, subcultural programming, by emphasizing content that people consider good, would reject undesirable content the moment there was evidence of its harmfulness.

The effects studies discussed in Chapter One indicate that the impact of any single item or even type of cultural content is negligible. Although more definitive research is still needed, the present evidence suggests that censorship of any kind is more harmful than the effects it purports to eliminate. Of course, people who feel that they or their children should not be exposed to violence, erotica, or other content which conflicts with their own values, have the freedom to practice private censorship, but they cannot demand that government or the media do it for them and deprive others of such content. Moreover, subcultural programming would add so much additional content to the cultural menu that everyone would have more choice and no one would be forced to choose what he or she considered undesirable because nothing else was available.

Fourth, insofar as subcultural programming accepts the right of taste publics to make their own aesthetic choices, it accepts the validity of user-oriented culture, and could thus be criticized for rejecting the priority of creator-oriented culture. Moreover, because creator-orientation is a principle of high culture, subcultural programming could be criticized for endangering that culture and for transforming yet more people from active creators into passive users.

Although user-oriented culture can be justified simply on the grounds that users of culture have as much right to satisfy their needs as do creators, subcultural programming would neither endanger high culture nor make users more passive. No evidence exists that the user-orientation is harmful to high culture, and subcultural programming would enhance the vitality of high culture through encouraging more diversity just as it would enhance the vitality of other taste cultures. Moreover, the creators most harmed by user-orientation are not those of high culture—they are well protected by its power and status, and its public aesthetic standards—but the creators of popular culture, whose artistic autonomy is sometimes restricted by the need to attract the largest possible audience. Subcultural programming would increase their autonomy, for greater diversity would make for smaller audiences for any single cultural product, allowing creators to find the audience who will accept their creative output.

Actually, high culture's attack on user-orientation is intended, as I noted earlier, to guarantee maximum resources for high culture creators, and to maximize the quantity and quality of high culture, in part so as to make a better cultural record for contemporary civilization as compared to past ones. The concern with societal taste levels and with intersocietal competitions is not a proper goal for public policy, however; the welfare and satisfaction of people now living is more important than a cultural record compiled for a nonexistent recordkeeper in a competition which is ultimately meaningless. Even if the culture of Elizabethan England were superior to that of contemporary America, it would be impossible to alter American society so as to recreate the society of Elizabethan England.

Accepting the validity of user-orientation will not make more people into passive users, because subcultural programming does not discourage people from being either amateur or trained creators, and insofar as it requires more cultural diversity, it will necessitate the recruitment of additional trained creators. Even so, condemning users as passive is an overly Calvinistic judgment which ignores the mental activity of users simply because they are physically passive, or are not producing a visible product.

The best solution is to emphasize neither users nor creators, but both. In an ideal situation, subcultural programming enables creators to do what they want and to create for the publics they wish to reach, while users are free to choose from the available content, and to be creators when they wish.

Fifth, because subcultural programming is aimed at specific taste publics rather than the population as a whole, it can be charged with introducing stratification and segregation into culture and rigidifying the taste hierarchy. Admittedly, subcultural programming would identify and legitimate the existence of individual taste publics, and, by meeting their needs, it would also create a set of cultures reflecting the taste hierarchy. It would not create such a hierarchy, however, but only make the existing one visible, although if resources flow equitably to all publics, that hierarchy would be served more equally and might be less unequal than it is today. Neither taste cultures nor taste publics would be segregated, however, for audience members would be as free as ever to choose whatever content they wish. Indeed, in some ways, there would be less segregation—and stratification—for people would have more diverse content from which to choose and could explore the offerings of more taste cultures.

Sixth, subcultural programming can be questioned for reducing the cohesive function of the mass media; their ability to focus the attention of the entire country on the same content at the same time. I doubt that this function is often served today, however, except in unusual situations such as the assassination of a president, when everyone watches the same television program. In addition, I doubt whether the mass media could significantly increase cohesion, for even if everyone saw the same television program or read the same magazine, each person would still perceive it from his or her own perspective. In a society split by differences of class and race, cohesion can probably only be increased when every group receives the resources it needs and thus sees that it has a common stake in the society. Subcultural programming, by providing at least some cultural resources, could thus help to encourage cohesion, although only to a limited extent. It can enhance equality by giving every taste public the equal right to achieve its aesthetic standards, but it cannot bring about the more basic forms of equality needed to make American society more cohesive.

Seventh, subcultural programming can be criticized on the ground that it would provide news and other informational content geared to the standards of each taste public, thus producing more of the often superficial informational content now offered to lower taste publics, and making it more difficult for them to function properly as citizens of a democratic society and to obtain the information needed to solve their own social or individual problems. In other words, subcultural programming might depress only further the current level of news and documentary broadcasting and writing.

142

To be sure, subculturally programmed news and other informational content would not be better by the conventional criteria, for it does not mean supplying all taste publics with the *New York Times* or its television equivalent, that is, the amount and kind of news now being used by high and upper-middle publics. Instead, subcultural programming means that each public would receive more information about those events in the total society that affect it most, so that, for example, news for the low public would emphasize what working-class people and institutions the country over were doing, and what was being done to them. As a result, people would be better informed about what concerns them most, and they might be more interested in the news than they are now.

Still, subcultural programming would probably not increase audience interest in news and other informational fare dramatically, and even if it did, the provision of better information—as I have defined it—would not dramatically alter the way people act in their personal or citizen roles. The effects data show that their actions are not much influenced by the mass media now, and the audience data indicate that demand for news and informational content is weaker than for entertainment.

The fact of the matter is that people are not receptacles who will accept any facts or ideas poured into them. Rather, people tend to act only on matters that concern them directly and they then select the kind of information they think is relevant to these matters, and to their values. As noted earlier, selective perception encourages them to reject or screen out information that violates these values. Although people are sometimes prey to insufficient and even false information as a result, they sometimes also seem to accept and even prefer misinformation. This is not meant to justify either supplying misinformation or restricting information altogether, but if people only hear what they want to hear,

143

alternate content will not reach them however loudly it is shouted. While this should not discourage shouting, it should also not inspire false confidence that shouting per se will be effective. Nor should these observations be interpreted to justify the censorship of facts or ideas, for it is always possible that someone will need or want such facts or ideas; I want only to make the point that facts, ideas, and other content are always strained through the sieves of cultural predisposition and selective perception.

Moreover, the extent to which people's predilections for insufficient or false information impair democracy deserves to be treated with less panic and more thought. Much anxiety over this issue stems from the historical formulation of American democracy; because it came into being in a time when the only citizens who really counted were the educated elite, democratic theory still assumes that all citizens must be educated on all issues. Nevertheless, democracies must and do function even when citizens are not educated. When people's interests are at stake, they generally act rationally despite being poorly educated and unable or unwilling to obtain proper information; or, rather, they act rationally with respect to their most important goals within the limits of the information available to them, although they may not be seeking the goals other people want them to seek. For example, while people may vote against their own economic interests, sometimes the cause is not lack of information but the existence of other goals which are of more importance to them than their economic interests. Moreover, their goals may conflict with the goals of other people, and the opposition of educated voters to uneducated ones often reflects an unrecognized difference in goals between them, a difference that the educated wrongly believe would disappear with better information. The uneducated voter's lack of personal interest in civil liberties for intellectuals would not be altered significantly if television were saturated with news and commentary on civil liberties. In a close election such saturation might swing enough votes to make a difference, but it would not alter the low interest in and relevance of the subject among many working- and lower-middle-class citizens. That can only be altered if and when the State attacks the civil liberties *they* consider important.

Subcultural news programming would raise information levels somewhat, but in addition, it is necessary to reevaluate the information requirements of democratic theory to determine what kinds of information, in what amounts and at what levels of analytic complexity, are essential for democracy and are effective in maintaining it. One would also need to know under what conditions people seek facts and ideas, particularly those questioning their own values, and I suspect that only when people are able and willing to participate more directly in politics will they be motivated to want different kinds of news coverage than at present. Meanwhile, it might be worthwhile to experiment with new ways of reporting facts and ideas, for example, through the fictional and quasi-fictional forms that seem to be popular with many taste publics. Popular television dramas which deal with one or more major domestic and foreign policy matters in the guise of fiction are worth trying, modeled on the old Lanny Budd novels by Upton Sinclair, or the more recent "non-fiction novel."[16]

Identifying the cultural content that people would use to help them solve individual and social problems may be even more difficult. People use culture not only for insight but also escape, and just entertainment, and while the high culture public is supposedly more willing to confront harsh reality, content that deals specifically with its problems and dilemmas is as rare in high culture as in others. *Waiting for Godot* may pose one of the basic existential dilemmas in modern society more adequately than a soap opera, but it does not offer much help to its audience in dealing with the dilemma as it pertains to their own life situation, and even if it did, I doubt whether the high culture public wants to confront its problems or stare reality in the face any more than any other public. For this reason, no taste culture is strongly inclined to pose harsh questions to its public or provide unpleasant ideas and facts, particularly when no solutions exist to significant problems. In high culture, the issues are often masked through abstraction and the use of symbolism; in popular taste cultures, through oversimplification, exaggeration and pseudorealism. But then people do not use culture—high or low—primarily to find solutions to their own and society's problems, and it would be naive to expect that subcultural programming would drastically alter the purposes and functions of culture.

Implementing Subcultural Programming

In theory, the implementation of subcultural programming requires three steps: (1) identifying all relevant taste publics and cultures and their aesthetic standards; (2) determining the publics which are currently poorly served with cultural content meeting their standards; and (3) creating the needed culture. For analytic purposes, it is useful to describe these three steps in somewhat more detail, although it must be emphasized that in real life, culture is not, cannot, and should not be created by such systematic planning procedures.

Identifying all the taste publics and their cultures is not an easy task, for as I indicated previously, they are not organized groups or systemic cultures, and even their standards are in large part unexpressed and uncodified. As a researcher, I can of course suggest a research program to make these identifications, and such a program would have three parts. One would be a thorough content analysis of all cultural products to determine which are similar and therefore cluster sufficiently so as to be considered taste cultures. The content analysis would look for similarities not only in substantive content, but also in structure, verbal and visual complexity, the values and assumptions that characterize the underlying world view of the product, and the aesthetic standards implicit in the product.[17]

The second part of the research program would be qualitative and quantitative studies of audience choices in all the media and the arts, to determine which kinds of people make what kinds of choices, and how these choices cluster. Intensive interviews would be needed to discover people's aesthetic standards; to find out what presently available cultural products—and what components of these products—they consider good or bad, and why; and to find out if and when people actually want to choose what they think is good. In addition, this part of the research program would also aim to discover, again through interviews, which publics are currently most poorly served by the mass (and class) media, who expresses a need or desire for more cultural fare, and, if possible, what the poorly served want in the way of additional culture. Of course, most people cannot tell researchers what they want, since they prefer to choose from what is available—and new and different—but those who are now poorly served may be able to indicate at least what gaps they feel exist.

The third part of the research program would combine and synthesize the first two; to relate clusters among cultures to clusters among choices and standards and then to determine which of these clusters are frequent and important enough to people, and sufficiently distinguishable from other clusters to delineate taste publics and cultures.

This research program would provide answers for the first two steps necessary to implement subcultural programming; but whether such research could actually be done and, if so, whether anyone would fund it is doubtful, and even then it is questionable whether creators would take it into consideration. At present, most creators resist exposure not only to the primitive kinds of audience research being used by the mass media, but to explicit feedback generally, for they argue that what satisfies them will also satisfy their eventual audience, and any intensive concern with audience demands would interfere with the creative process. Media decision makers are less reluctant to use audience research, however, although they still have difficulty in getting creators to pay attention to research findings.

The creators' reluctance is understandable, for creation is, even in the mass media, a personal act, and difficult enough without the further complexity that would be introduced by information about audience standards and preferences. Nevertheless, much of the conflict between creators and decision makers in popular culture is about what the audience will accept, and it could be resolved more intelligently if proper audience research were available. Nor would such research stifle creativity, for even the most comprehensive research program cannot uncover what Eric Larrabee has called "the hidden, half-formed and yet unsatisfied . . . public wants."[18] It can only tell creators and decision makers what the audience has chosen in the past, and with what degree of enthusiasm, but the data on past choices and present wants can never be directly applied to the creation of new content. As one newsmagazine editor once told me, research about what magazine covers people like will show a consistent preference for a pretty girl on a red background, but no newsmagazine can publish red covers with pretty girls week after week. Novelty and surprise are essential qualities of all art and entertainment, both for creators and audiences, and research cannot provide them.

The third step in the plan would be the actual creation of new culture, but this is even more a planner's fantasy than the previously mentioned research program, for culture is not often created through systematic planning. New cultural fare seems to come into being when creators and users are dissatisfied with the existing fare, and when it no longer responds to their wants, as suggested by the cultural innovations on the part of young people and racial minorities described in Chapter Two. This process also seems far more desirable than the kind of systematic planning I outlined above, which is likely to be elitist even when people are consulted through audience research. This is not to say that culture can only be created on a laissez-faire basis; even when people are not unhappy with their present fare, innovations in culture can be stimulated by the provision of funds and the recruitment and training of creative people, but whatever planning takes place should emphasize participatory methods over those dominated by the decision making of experts.

PROGRAMMING FOR THE POORLY SERVED

Probably the only practical way to bring about subcultural programming is to identify very generally which taste publics are now poorly served, and then to find ways of encouraging existing and new creators, and media, to go to work. The identification of poorly served publics is a major empirical task itself, but even an impressionistic survey points to some very real gaps. As I noted earlier, the poor, the old, and racial and ethnic minorities are not well served by the existing media, and not only on television. There are now too few newspapers and magazines which provide information relevant to their social situation, and fiction, whether in print or film form, is also scarce. In fact, low culture and quasi-folk culture are in short supply, and for working-class people as well as for the poor. Cultural fare for the middle-aged is also scarce, and for single people other than the affluent customers of the new singles market. Much of today's popular culture is suburban; very little deals with central city, rural, or small-town themes, and America's regions, other than the East and Far West are commonly ignored as well. Some of these groups may be satisfied with using culture created for other groups; for example, some old and middle-aged people may prefer to watch and read about the activities of youthful fictional characters, but those with different preferences have no other choice.

The situation in art is even more dismal; most publicly available art is high or upper-middle in culture, or lower-middle adaptation thereof. Low culture religious art can still be purchased in religious stores, but secular low culture art is scarcer. Different kinds of music are more widely available, for the economics of the music industry make it possible for variety to be made available through all-music radio stations and records, although not everyone can afford to buy the latter. Even so, the music that was once supplied by band concerts or by Lawrence Welk on network television is rare today, and people who prefer "swing" and other kinds of popular music of the 1940s and 1950s must wait for a nostalgic revival to meet their needs.

In addition to poorly served users, there may also be poorly served creators. Obviously, some creators enjoy better working conditions than others, and I suspect that low culture creators are sometimes the most regimented. In addition, creators with new ideas do not have easy access to the mass media, for media recruitment processes are so highly institutionalized that people with new ideas are often kept out, even when media decision makers are complaining about a shortage of innovators. To be sure, most of the self-styled innovators who want access to the media offer inferior imitations of the existing fare, and some original creators who cannot gain access to national media enrich the cultural lives of their friends and neighbors with their new ideas, but it is nevertheless true that the local music halls, and night-clubs, and the low-budget movie companies which once existed to exhibit and train new talent have disappeared, and the highly bureaucratized national media with high overhead are often reluctant to take risks with new ideas and new talent.

Identifying the poorly served users is easier than serving them. For one thing, many of them are also poorly paid and cannot afford anything but "free" television. Even if their financial problems were solved, a major structural and economic obstacle would remain. Subcultural programming would require a change in the structure of the media, for they would have to create cultural fare for more narrowly demarcated audiences, and thus for smaller ones. Either the existing media would need to decentralize, or new media would have to be added. For example, instead of three television network news departments and three newsmagazines, each competing for much the same audience, six to twelve might be necessary, with each seeking to attract different publics, although competition for the same publics need not be avoided. In fact, it would be undesirable for any one network or magazine to monopolize a single public.

Once subcultural programming, even for only the now poorly served publics, is implemented, present feedback mechanisms and some additional audience research could subsequently determine the success of the new programming efforts and incorporate its findings into further content creation through trial and error. If, in addition, trained critics who judge culture by the standards of individual taste publics could be recruited—and paid—their criticism would provide additional feedback to the media.

Recruiting new critics and creators will be less difficult than to change the existing media or to establish new ones, for subcultural programming is not likely to be profitable, at least in the short run. It would be more expensive than present programming, for it would require more content distributed in a more decentralized fashion to smaller audiences, and in some cases to audiences who could not afford to pay for their cultural fare either directly or indirectly. Moreover, subcultural programming would have to compete with the existing media, and would therefore have to be of equal technical quality, so that production costs would be just as high.

In the long run, subcultural programming might become profitable, for if it met audience needs more adequately than the present fare, the size of the total audience might increase, or the sales potential of the advertisers' commercials might rise. While the cost of reaching a thousand viewers or readers would probably never be as low as in the existing media, the thousand viewers might be more satisfied and might thus pay more attention to the advertiser's message. Incorporating the now poorly served audiences into the "media economy" might also increase advertisers' sales and might even attract some new advertisers. Still, low income people could not be supplied with more culture on a profitable basis, and even subcultural programming for more affluent publics would require initial subsidies to develop new media, recruit creators, and attract audiences.

There is, of course, no intrinsic reason why popular culture must be created and distributed solely by profit-making firms. Nonprofit organizations have always participated in the creation and distribution of high culture, and in recent years, some have taken an active role in youth culture and black culture. Even so, most nonprofit cultural activities have been small in scale, and the most prudent prediction would be that if subcultural programming is to appear, it will be provided largely by trained professionals working largely in profit-seeking organizations, or in relatively large nonprofit agencies such as public television.

FINANCING SUBCULTURAL PROGRAMMING

Nevertheless, someone has to pay even for nonprofit ventures, and there are only four possible sources of financing subcultural programming: the audience, advertisers, the existing media, or the general public, that is, the government. Given the audience's lack of intensive involvement with current mass media fare, I doubt that it would be willing to pay much for most subcultural programming as long as it can obtain other programming "free" or at lower cost. Advertisers would eventually be attracted, but it is questionable whether they would be able or willing to sponsor cultural innovations for small audiences as long as they can reach large audiences through the existing programming. In theory, there is no reason why the existing media cannot be asked to institute subcultural innovation, or to provide funds to new subcultural media out of their often high profits. The television networks provided such funds to public television when it was in its infancy, partly to gain prestige, partly to be relieved of the unprofitable burden of programming for the upper-middle public. In practice, however, asking the media to help is not likely to work, since no one, including the government, is powerful enough to make them alter their present activities or to divert some of their profits to innovation or to other media.

Ultimately, then, the government is probably the most feasible source of funds, either by subsidizing media intent on providing subcultural programming, or by supplying such programming through government-owned media, as is the case in Europe. Each alternative has advantages and disadvantages, but some generic problems develop when government begins to participate in cultural creation, for it is rarely inclined to aid political opponents, fund controversial programming, or even support freedom of the press when it is politically disadvantageous. These drawbacks pertain especially to government-owned media, which will generally try to use their programming to generate support for the politicians and parties in power. Government subsidy of privately owned media is not without problems either, as the difficulty of public television in obtaining federal funds for news and other programming with political implications illustrates. Still, government is already creating culture of sorts through its public relations and educational activities, and it is now subsidizing public television, universities, libraries, and other cultural institutions which cater primarily to an upper-middle public, providing sufficient justification for the argument that it should also subsidize cultural creation for less affluent publics.

Probably the best solution is to restrict government's role to providing grants to subcultural programmers, and to limit such grants to programmers who want to reach publics too small or too poor to be served by the commercial media. One approach might be to establish grant-giving offices within agencies which now support cultural activities, for example, the National Endowment for the Humanities and the Office of Education, although poor audiences which are being ignored by the commercial media would probably be better served by a granting office located in a federal anti-poverty agency. Grants to fund programming for the aged might be provided by existing federal agencies concerned with the problems of the elderly; for children, by various offices within Health, Education, and Welfare which now look after their needs. This approach may run into two kinds of difficulties: the inability or unwillingness of some of these agencies to oversee the provision of culture, and particularly popular culture; and the political fact that new ideas for government spending are more feasible if they benefit a larger proportion of the population. For example, while the Endowment for the Humanities is qualified to give grants to support high and upper-middle culture activities, its present cultural values limit its qualifications for subsidizing low culture; and the Office of Education has traditionally been reluctant to draw on popular culture approaches even for educational purposes.

The political difficulty is even harder to deal with;

154

although the government has generally been able to initiate new activities for the aged and for children, the poor are politically less popular. Consequently, a second alternative might be an across-the-board funding scheme for all parts of the population, to be based on a certain amount per year for every person in the country. For instance, if the government appropriated only five dollars per person a year, over one billion dollars would be available annually for this purpose, and the amount would grow as the population increased in size.

These monies could go to a new independent agency, somewhat like the Corporation for Public Broadcasting, but with a very different policy-making board. Such a board would not be recruited from the businessmen and civic leaders who now become trustees for independent agencies; its members would have to include creators and users from all taste publics, so that all would share in the allocation of funds, particularly publics that are poorly served by the present media. Of course, no independent agency funded by a government is ever truly independent, and the allocation of funds is likely to follow the election returns and to reflect the demands of powerful politicians, so that powerless minorities such as the poor would probably fare badly. On this count, at least, having programming funds distributed by agencies already responsible for and to specific populations would be more desirable.

Even so, neither a new agency nor existing agencies are likely to offer grants for controversial programming, or for programming which could arouse the ire of powerful politicians. Such programming would have to be created by agencies outside the government, as it is now, including private foundations. The foundations might be encouraged to spend more money on subcultural programming by special tax incentives, but even they are not immune to political pressure, and controversial culture will continue to be created

155

and funded by individual creators operating on a shoestring, and more important, by political and social movements. Young people, blacks and other minorities have been culturally innovative without governmental aid, and as I noted earlier, the strongest impetus to cultural innovation is a widely felt need for new culture, and while that impetus can be aided with public subsidies, it is likely to persist even without them.

The Outlook for More
Cultural Pluralism

The likelihood that any of these proposals would be implemented is small. Since most mass media are still profitable, they have little incentive to change, and they have enough power to discourage government efforts to make them change. Nor is government likely to act, for it, too, lacks incentives to alter the status quo. It would act if audiences organized to demand change, but not enough people are sufficiently dissatisfied with the existing cultural fare, or well enough organized even when they are dissatisfied. Moreover, few people have sufficient trust in government to exert political pressure for government intervention in matters of culture, for they are frightened, and rightly so, of government attempts to harass journalists and the news media, and besides, there is no tradition in America for using political pressure to bring about government participation in cultural creation.

Subcultural programming may come into being for other reasons, however, through the existing media and by spontaneous cultural innovation, although not in the comprehensive way I have suggested. Some subcultural programming has always existed, notably in book publishing, with different publishers catering to different taste publics; and it is increasing in magazine publishing, where periodicals aimed at specific age groups and interests are rapidly supplanting the general magazines; as well as in the movie industry, which now only rarely makes the costly spectaculars intended to attract the largest possible audience.

A slight trend toward subcultural programming is even noticeable in television, which in the past has programmed less for diverse audiences than have the other mass media. Ever since some advertisers discovered that they could best sell their wares by reaching potential buyers rather than the largest number of viewers, they have been interested in programs that appeal to specific age, sex, and sometimes even income groups in the total audience. Although this is subcultural advertising, it has had some effect on programming as well, at least within the lower-middle taste public to which television primarily caters. Even so, the resulting additional diversity has been modest; television still appeals largely to young adults of median and above-median income, and there is currently no programming for old people or for the poor and near-poor. Public television has created a national network for upper-middle cultural fare, with some programs devoted to children from other taste publics, notably "Sesame Street" and "The Electric Company." Technological innovations such as UHF and CATV have made available additional television channels which could be used to broadcast to many different publics. The latest invention is cassette television, which allows individual viewers to choose their own programs at home, enabling each to select his or her own subculture. Programming the new outlets has been slow so far, however, partly because no one knows what market exists for further television programming, or whether any market exists at all, except for sports or popular spectaculars which are withdrawn from "free" television. Because of their cost, CATV and cassettes can at best only expand subcultural programming among the affluent in any case, and UHF channels attract so small an

157

audience in most cities that they are, so far at least, of minor significance. In the future, however, they may be the best resource for programming for less affluent taste publics, provided, of course, that enough funds are available to create programs which can compete with network fare.

All of these tendencies are likely to become stronger in the years to come. Further technological improvements are already making filming, televising, and printing cheaper and simpler, so that economically, further subcultural programming is not out of the question, at least for the affluent. For example, recent technological simplifications in film and television cameras and videotape machines have already made it possible for small and nonprofit film and television companies to make very low budget films and programs, although they have not had much success in obtaining access to movie theaters and television screens, at least on major channels.

Nevertheless, the strongest stimulus for more cultural pluralism will come from the users of culture. The continued existence of social and political movements among racial and ethnic minorities, women, adolescents, young adults, blue collar workers, and others and their rising interest in new roles and identities is likely to enhance both their need for new culture and their cultural creativity. In addition, the growing diversity of interests and the search for new means of self-expression among much of the rest of the population, together with the possibility of more leisure time in the future if the workday or the workweek are reduced, may also create a greater demand for more and more diverse culture. The increase in vacations and the proliferation of three- and four-day weekends has already stimulated a rise in travel—and with it a new growth in "tourist culture"—as well as a sharp upturn in the sale of summer homes, boats, skis, snowmobiles, and camping equipment. In fact, the principal growth may take place in outdoor rather than indoor culture, and in participatory rather than spectator activities.

None of these tendencies holds much promise for the less affluent, however; even the new black and youth cultures serve mainly the affluent, and although the poor and near-poor need subcultural programming the most, they are least likely to get it. These groups are by now used to being deprived, even if they are not happy about it, and besides, better jobs and higher incomes are of more urgent priority than culture. As for the rest of the population, it has the commercial and political power to demand more subcultural programming, but only time will tell whether culture is of sufficient importance to it to bring such programming into existence.

Notes

INTRODUCTION
Mass Culture, Popular Culture, and Taste Culture

1. Leo Lowenthal and Marjorie Fiske, "The Debate Over Art and Popular Culture in Eighteenth Century England," in Mirra Komarovsky, ed., *Common Frontiers of the Social Sciences* (Glencoe, Ill.: The Free Press, 1957), pp. 33-96.

2. Nathan Glazer, "The Role of the Intellectuals," *Commentary* 53 (February 1971): 55-61, quote on p. 57.

3. Daniel Bell, "The Cultural Contradictions of Capitalism," *The Public Interest*, no. 21 (Fall 1970): 16-43, quote on pp. 19-20. See also his *The Coming of Post-Industrial Society* (New York: Basic Books, 1973), particularly pp. 475-486.

4. For a description of the new egalitarianism, see Herbert J. Gans, *More Equality* (New York: Pantheon Books, 1973), particularly chapters 1 and 2.

5. For one critique of equality in terms of its effects on culture, see Bertrand de Jouvenal, "The Ethics of Redistribution," in Edward C. Budd, ed., *Inequality and Poverty* (New York: Norton, 1967), pp. 6-13.

6. For a thoughtful statement of this argument, see Daniel Bell, "Meritocracy and Equality," *The Public Interest* no. 29 (Fall 1972): 29-68, particularly pp. 65-66.

7. Dwight MacDonald, "A Theory of Mass Culture," in Bernard Rosenberg and David M. White, eds., *Mass Culture: The Popular Arts in America* (Glencoe, Ill.: Free Press, 1957), pp. 59-73, quote on p. 59.

8. The distinction between partial and total cultures is explored further in Chapter Two, pp. 95-97.

9. The results of effects research are discussed in more detail in Chapter One, pp. 31-43.

10. See, for example, John G. Cawelti, "Notes Toward an Aesthetic of Popular Culture," *Journal of Popular Culture* 5 (Fall 1971): 255-268; and David Madden, "The Necessity for an Aesthetics of Popular Culture," *Journal of Popular Culture* 7 (Summer 1973): 1-13.

CHAPTER ONE
The Critique of Mass Culture

1. The principal statements of the critique are presented in two books. The first is Bernard Rosenberg and David M. White, eds., *Mass Culture: The Popular Arts in America* (Glencoe, Ill.: The Free Press, 1957), particularly the articles by Bernard Rosenberg, Jose Ortega y Gasset, Leo Lowenthal, Dwight MacDonald, Clement Greenberg, T. W. Adorno, Marshall McLuhan, Irving Howe, Ernest van den Haag, Leslie Fiedler, and Melvin Tumin. The second book is Norman Jacobs, ed., *Culture for the Millions* (Princeton, N.J.: Van Nostrand, 1961), particularly the articles by Hannah Arendt, Ernest van den Haag, Oscar Handlin, Randall Jarrell, and Stanley Edgar Hyman. See also T. S. Eliot, *Notes Towards the Definition of Culture* (New York: Harcourt, Brace, 1949), and the work of F. R. Leavis, for example, F. R. Leavis and Denys Thompson, *Culture and Environment* (London: Chatto and Windus, 1937).

2. The most pervasive, albeit implicit, rebuttal of the mass culture critique is to be found in David Riesman's sympathetic and empathic analysis of popular culture. See David Riesman, with Reuel Denney and Nathan Glazer, *The Lonely Crowd* (New Haven: Yale University Press, 1950) particularly chapters 4 and 5, and David Riesman, *Individualism Reconsidered* (Glencoe, Ill.: The Free Press, 1954) part 4. The best empirically based rebuttal of the charges against mass culture is Raymond A. Bauer and Alice H. Bauer, "American Mass Society and Mass Media," *Journal of Social Issues* 16, no. 3 (1960): 3-66. See also Joseph Klapper, *The Effects of Mass Communication* (New York: The Free Press of Glencoe, 1960); Wilbur Schramm. ed., *The Science of Communication* (New York: Basic Books, 1963); and Edward Shils, "The Mass Society and Its Culture," in Jacobs, *Culture for the Millions*, pp. 1-27.

3. On this problem, see Paul Lazarsfeld, "Afterword," in Gary Steiner, *The People Look at Television* (New York: Alfred A. Knopf, 1963), pp. 409-422.

4. Leo Lowenthal, "Historical Perspectives of Popular Culture," in Rosenberg and White, *Mass Culture*, p. 55.

5. Dwight MacDonald, "A Theory of Mass Culture," in Rosenberg and White, *Mass Culture*, p. 55.

6. The implications of audience size are discussed by Rolf Meyersohn, "A Critical Examination of Commercial Entertainment," in Robert W. Kleemeier, ed., *Aging and Leisure* (New York: Oxford University Press, 1961), pp. 243-272, especially pp. 254ff.

7. See, for example, the late Hugh Dalziel Duncan's brilliant analysis of the relationship between creators, audiences, and critics in his *Language and Literature in Society* (Chicago: University of Chicago Press, 1953) particularly chapter 4.

8. Two experimental studies of creator-audience relationships have become classics: Raymond A. Bauer, "The Communicator and His Audience," and Ithiel De Sola Pool and Irwin Shulman, "Newsmen's Fantasies, Audiences and News-

writing," both in Lewis A. Dexter and David M. White, eds., *People, Society and Mass Communications* (New York: Free Press, 1964), pp. 125-140 and 141-159 respectively. Among organizational analyses of the creator-audience relationship, see Paul M. Hirsch, "Processing Fads and Fashions," *American Journal of Sociology* 77 (January 1972): 639-659; and Edward J. Epstein, *News from Nowhere* (New York: Random House, 1973). My own work is described in more detail in "The Creator Audience Relationship: An Analysis of Movie-Making," in Rosenberg and White, *Mass Culture*, pp. 315-324, and "How Well Does Television Cover the News?" *New York Times Magazine* 119 (January 11, 1970): 30-45.

9. For more detail, see Muriel Cantor, *The Hollywood Producer* (New York: Basic Books, 1971).

10. The distinction between creator-orientation and user-orientation intersects at points with Riesman's distinction between inner-direction and other-direction, particularly insofar as Riesman identifies craftsmanship with the former. My concepts refer primarily to roles people play in popular culture, however, and presumably, both creators and users can be either inner-directed or other-directed. See Riesman, Denney, and Glazer, *The Lonely Crowd*. Duncan describes what I call creator-orientation as the defense of "craft principles." See Hugh D. Duncan, *Symbols in Society* (New York: Oxford University Press, 1968), p. 196. For good illustrations of creator and user differences and conflicts, see Howard S. Becker, "The Professional Dance Musician and His Audience," *American Journal of Sociology* 57 (September 1951): 136-144, and Robert Faulkner, *Hollywood Studio Musicians* (Chicago: Aldine-Atherton, 1971).

11. Faulkner, *Hollywood Studio Musicians*, chapter 3.

12. Ernest van den Haag, "Of Happiness and Despair We Have No Measure," in Rosenberg and White, *Mass Culture*, pp. 524-525.

13. Some of the studio musicians studied by Faulkner spent a good deal of their remaining working hours playing chamber music and other high culture works, or teaching in schools training classical musicians. However, this "bicultural" activity is easier for a performer than for a composer.

14. MacDonald, in Rosenberg and White, *Mass Culture*, p. 72.

15. Van den Haag, in Rosenberg and White, *Mass Culture*, p. 529.

16. Among recent community studies of the poor, see Kenneth Clark, *Dark Ghetto* (New York: Harper & Row, 1965); Elliot Liebow, *Tally's Corner* (Boston: Little Brown, 1967); Lee Rainwater, *Behind Ghetto Walls* (Chicago: Aldine, 1970); and Carol B. Stack, *All Our Kin* (New York: Harper & Row, 1974). Among the major mental health studies are August B. Hollingshead and Frederick C. Redlich, *Social Class and Mental Illness* (New York: John Wiley and Sons, 1958) and Thomas S. Langner and Stanley T. Michael, *Life Stress and Mental Health* (New York: The Free Press of Glencoe, 1963).

17. See, for example, Bradley S. Greenberg and Brenda Dervin, *Use of the Mass Media by the Urban Poor* (New York: Praeger, 1970).

18. Langner and Michael, *Life Stress*.

19. According to one study, there has been a decline in mental illness over the last hundred years. See Herbert Goldhamer and Andrew M. Marshall, *Psychosis and Civilization* (Glencoe, Ill.: The Free Press, 1953).

20. Among the principal studies are Matilda Riley and John W. Riley, "A Sociological Approach to Communications Research," *Public Opinion Quarterly* 15 (Fall 1951): 445-460, and Elihu Katz and Paul Lazarsfeld, *Personal Influence* (Glencoe, Ill.: The Free Press, 1955).

21. Eliot Freidson, "Communications Research and the Concept of the Mass," *American Sociological Review* 18 (June 1953): 313-317.

22. For one illustration, see Herbert J. Gans, *The Urban Villagers* (New York: The Free Press of Glencoe, 1962), chapter 9.

23. Klapper, *Effects of Mass Communication*. See also Rolf Meyersohn, "Social Research in Television," in Rosenberg and White, *Mass Culture*, pp. 245-257.

24. See Robert Baker and Sandra J. Ball, *Violence and the Media: A Staff Report to the National Commission on the Causes and Prevention of Violence* (Washington: Government Printing Office, November 1969) and Surgeon General's Advisory Committee, *Television and Growing Up: The Impact of Televised Violence* (Washington: Government Printing Office, 1972), 5 volumes. For a detailed analysis of the latter, see Leo Bogart, "Warning: The Surgeon General Has Determined That Television Violence Is Moderately Dangerous to Your Child's Mental Health," *Public Opinion Quarterly* 36 (Winter 1972-1973): 491-522, and Herbert J. Gans, "Media Violence and Its Effects," *Social Policy* 3 (July-August 1972): 58-61. One study, based on research in a natural field setting, even suggests that media violence may help to reduce aggressive behavior. See Seymour Feshbach and Robert D. Singer, *Television and Aggression* (San Francisco: Jossey-Bass, 1971). For earlier effects studies, see particularly H. Himmelweit, A. Oppenheim, and P. Vance, *Television and the Child* (London: Oxford University Press, 1958); W. Schramm, J. Lyle, and E. Parker, *Television in the Lives of Our Children* (Stanford: Stanford University Press, 1961); and Walter Weiss, "Effects of the Mass Media of Communication," in Gardner Lindzey and Elliott Aronson, eds., *Handbook of Social Psychology* 2nd ed. (Reading, Mass: Addison-Wesley, 1969), vol. 5, pp. 77-195.

25. See, for example, Daniel Bell, "The Myth of Crime Waves," in his *End of Ideology* (Glencoe, Ill.: The Free Press, 1960), chapter 8, and Theodore N. Ferdinand, "The Criminal Patterns of Boston Since 1849," *American Journal of Sociology* 73 (July 1967): 84-99.

26. *The Report of the Commission on Obscenity and Pornography* (New York: Bantam Books, 1970), especially pp. 169-309.

27. Van den Haag, in Rosenberg and White, *Mass Culture* pp. 533-534.

28. Herta Herzog, "Motivations and Gratifications of Daily Serial Listeners," in Wilbur Schramm, ed., *The Process and Effects of Mass Communications* (Urbana: University of Illinois Press, 1955), pp. 50-55. See also Herbert J. Gans, *The Uses of Television and Their Educational Implications* (New York: Center for Urban Education, 1968).

29. Eliot Freidson, "Adult Discount: An Aspect of Children's Changing Taste," *Child Development* 24 (March 1953): 39-49. See also David Riesman, with Evelyn T. Riesman, "Movies and Audiences," in Riesman, *Individualism Reconsidered*, pp. 194-201.

30. For an early and still relevant analysis of this point see Riesman, Denney, and Glazer, *The Lonely Crowd*, pp. 225-234. See also Bauer and Bauer, "American Mass Society," p. 53 and Bernard Cohen, *The Press and Foreign Policy* (Princeton: Princeton University Press, 1963).

31. Gans, *Uses of Television*.

32. Klapper, *Effects of Mass Communication*.

33. P. Lazarsfeld, B. Berelson, and H. Gaudet, *The People's Choice* (New York: Columbia University Press, 1948) and B. Berelson, P. Lazarsfeld, and W. McPhee, *Voting* (Chicago: University of Chicago Press, 1954). On the debates, see Elihu Katz and Jacob Feldman, "The Debates in the Light of Research," in S. Kraus, ed., *The Great Debates* (Bloomington, Ind.: University of Indiana Press, 1962), pp. 173-223 and Kurt Lang and Gladys Engel Lang, *Politics and Television* (Chicago: Quadrangle Books, 1968), particularly chapter 6.

34. Steven H. Chaffee, "National Election Campaigns as a Vehicle for Testing Major Hypotheses About Communication," unpublished paper (February 1974), p. 9. For an empirical demonstration of agenda-setting, see Maxwell McCombs and Donald Shaw, "The Agenda-setting Function of Mass Media," *Public Opinion Quarterly* 36 (Summer 1972): 176-187.

35. For an excellent analysis that emphasizes the role of sources in the determination of news coverage, see Harvey Molotch and Marilyn Lester, "News As Purposive Behavior: On the Strategic Use of Routine Events, Accidents and Scandals," *American Sociological Review* 39 (February 1974): 101-112.

36. The principal statement of this part of the critique is in José Ortega y Gasset, *Revolt of the Masses* (New York: Norton, 1932). See also his "The Coming of the Masses," in Rosenberg and White, *Mass Culture*, pp. 41-45.

37. Bernard Rosenberg, "Mass Culture in America," in Rosenberg and White, *Mass Culture*, pp. 3-12, quote on p. 9.

38. Herbert Marcuse, "Repressive Tolerance," in R. Wolff, B. Moore, Jr., and H. Marcuse, *A Critique of Pure Tolerance* (Boston: Beacon Press, 1969), p. 95. See also his *One Dimensional Man* (Boston: Beacon Press, 1964).

39. Jacques Ellul, *Propaganda: The Formation of Men's Attitudes* (New York: Vintage, 1973), particularly chapter 3. Ellul's inclusion of mass culture in propaganda is noted only in a footnote on p. 110.

40. Paul F. Lazarsfeld and Robert K. Merton, "Mass Communication, Popular Taste and Organized Social Action," in Rosenberg and White, *Mass Culture*, pp. 457-473, especially p. 467. See also the excellent critique of the declining taste-level charge in Bauer and Bauer, "American Mass Society," pp. 42ff.

41. William Kornhauser, *The Politics of Mass Society* (Glencoe, Ill.: The Free Press, 1959).

42. Bauer and Bauer, "American Mass Society," pp. 56ff.

43. Marcuse, "Repressive Tolerance," p. 100.

44. I am indebted to Peter Marris for many of the ideas in this paragraph.

45. On the political attitudes of some conservative critics, see, for example, William M. Chace, *The Political Identities of Ezra Pound and T. S. Eliot* (Stanford: Stanford University Press, 1973) and David Craig, *The Real Foundations: Literature and Social Change* (New York: Oxford University Press, 1973). On the

Frankfurt school of critics, see Martin Jay, *The Dialectical Imagination* (Boston: Little Brown, 1973), chapter 4.

46. Their ambivalence about cultural democracy is clearly expressed in a panel discussion in Jacobs, *Culture for the Millions*, pp. 155ff.

47. Edward Shils, "Daydreams and Nightmares: Reflections on the Criticism of Mass Culture," *Sewanee Review* 65 (1957): 587-608.

48. Daniel Lerner, *The Passing of Traditional Society* (Glencoe, Ill.: The Free Press, 1958).

49. Edward Shils, "Mass Society and Its Culture," in Jacobs, *Culture for the Millions*, p. 1.

50. See, for example, Martha Wolfenstein and Nathan Leites, *Movies: A Psychological Study* (Glencoe, Ill.: Free Press, 1950).

51. For some evidence that women do not imitate the ideas of the homemaking magazines, see Herbert J. Gans, *The Levittowners* (New York: Pantheon Books, 1967), pp. 191-192.

52. Edward Shils, "Panel Discussion," in Jacobs, *Culture for the Millions*, pp. 198-199. Incidentally, Shils is one of the few conservative intellectuals who does not endorse the mass culture critique. Even so, he does not approve of mass culture, and appears to condemn the critics of mass culture mainly for being "broken down Trotskyites and *Edelmarxisten*." Shils, *The Intellectuals and the Powers and Other Essays* (Chicago: University of Chicago Press, 1972), p. xi. Shils' antipathy to Marxism is intense enough to make him forget that the mass culture critique was actually first formulated by conservatives.

53. See Lyman Bryson, *The Next America* (New York: Harper & Brothers, 1952), especially chapter 17.

CHAPTER TWO
A Comparative Analysis of High and Popular Culture

1. The Selznicks describe this as "the strain toward the aesthetic." Gertrude Selznick and Philip Selznick, "A Normative Theory of Culture," *American Sociological Review* 29 (October 1964): 653-669, quote on p. 664. See also Hugh D. Duncan, *Symbols and Social Theory* (New York: Oxford University Press, 1969), part 2.

2. These are hypothetical descriptions, for although there is considerable market research on the interrelations of choice, most of it remains confidential and little academic research has been done in this subject area. The pioneer study is W. Lloyd Warner and Paul S. Lunt, *The Social Life of a Modern Community* (New Haven: Yale University Press, 1941), especially chapter 19. See also August B. Hollingshead and Frederick C. Redlich, *Social Class and Mental Illness* (New York: John Wiley and Sons, 1958), appendix 3, pp. 398-407. For a study which tested my concept of taste culture among young people, see R. Denisoff and M. Levine, "Youth and Popular Music," *Youth and Society* 4 (December 1972): 237-255.

3. Van Wyck Brooks, *America's Coming of Age* (Garden City, N.Y.: Anchor Books, Doubleday, 1958) and Russell Lynes, "Highbrow, Middlebrow, Lowbrow," in *The Tastemakers* (New York: Harper & Brothers, 1954), chapter 13.

4. This notion is explored further in Herbert J. Gans, "Diversity and Homogeneity in American Culture" in *People and Plans* (New York: Basic Books, 1968), chapter 11.

5. I use class here not in the Marxist sense of an organized or potentially organized interest group but as a synonym for socioeconomic level. Whatever one's opinion on the existence of classes in American society, taste publics are not classes but aggregates of people who are similar on one or more of the three major indices of class position. However, what sociologists call *status inconsistency*, that is, the lack of consistency between the three sociological indices of class, is probably more frequent for cultural choices than for most other behavior patterns, partly because education is the most important factor in determining taste. For example, a rich person who earned his money in a low status business and attended school for only ten years is likely to belong to a low taste public even though his other behavior choices will reflect his income.

6. Edward Shils, who maintains the tripartite division used by Brooks and Lynes, uses the terms *refined, mediocre,* and *brutal,* which are hardly neutral. See Edward Shils, "The Mass Society and Its Culture," in Norman Jacobs, ed., *Culture for the Millions* (Princeton, N.J.: Van Nostrand, 1961), pp. 1-27.

7. Another alternative would be to use the modal educational level of each public, thus calling them *university, collegiate, high school, tenth grade,* and *grade school.*

8. Daniel Bell, "The Cultural Contradictions of Capitalism," *The Public Interest* no. 2 (Fall 1970): 16-43 and Hilton Kramer, "The Rise and Fall of the Avant-Grade," *Commentary* 54 (October 1972): 37-45.

9. Hugh Dalziel Duncan, *Language and Literature in Society* (Chicago: University of Chicago Press, 1953), p. 65. Actually, creators also determine aesthetic standards, but since neither they nor the critics have unilateral power to set standards, they sometimes fight each other to determine what is or is not high culture, and who should decide these issues.

10. Susan Sontag, "Notes on 'Camp,' " *Partisan Review* 31 (Fall 1964): 515-531. For a description of the consumption of camp and an example of how new high culture trends are reported for upper-middle-class publics, see Thomas Meehan, "Not Good Taste, Not Bad Taste; It's Camp," *New York Times Magazine* 114 (March 21, 1965): 30-31, 113-115. In my analytic scheme, camp was a temporary subfaction and fashion in avant-grade high culture, especially among its homosexual public.

11. Much of Riesman's analysis of popular culture deals with upper-middle culture, and many of his conclusions are still relevant today. See Riesman, Denney, and Glazer, *The Lonely Crowd.*

12. The boundaries of conventional upper-middle culture may be discernable in the fate of *Harper's* magazine during the editorship of Willie Morris and his colleagues. Their changes in the magazine, partly in a more progressive upper-

middle, partly in a more high culture, direction, resulted in a loss of circulation and Morris's eventual resignation. The two young entrepreneurs from *Psychology Today* who bought the *Saturday Review* from Norman Cousins also attempted to move the magazine in a progressive direction, particularly in style, and went bankrupt, enabling Cousins, who may be prototypical of conventional upper-middle culture, to regain ownership and control of the magazine.

13. For a good illustration of lower-middle attitudes toward and participation in culture, see National Research Center of the Arts, *Arts and the People* mimeographed (New York: Cranford-Wood, 1973). This study, conducted by Louis Harris and Associates, provides data concerning the use of and attitudes toward a variety of cultural facilities, and since the data are broken down by income and education, they suggest the extent of interest in many high and upper-middle cultural facilities among the lower-middle public, particularly young people.

14. Lester Asheim, "From Book to Film," *Quarterly of Film, Radio and Television* 5 (1950): 289-349 and 6 (1951): 54-68, 258-273. See also George Bluestone, *Novels into Film* (Baltimore: Johns Hopkins Press, 1957).

15. One reason they shun the critics is that the critics tend to defend upper-middle culture standards. See Jules J. Wanderer, "In Defense of Popular Taste: Film Ratings Among Professionals and Lay Audiences," *American Journal of Sociology* 76 (September 1970): 262-272.

16. Herbert J. Gans, *The Urban Villagers* (New York: The Free Press of Glencoe, 1962), chapters 3 and 11.

17. Ibid., Chapter 9.

18. For a somewhat similar classification, see Jesse Pitts, "The Counter Culture," *Dissent* 18 (June 1971): 216-229. Writers advocating these cultures have published extensively, for example, Ken Kesey on the drug-and-music culture; Tom Hayden on the political culture; and Abbie Hoffman and Jerry Rubin on the neo-dadaist culture. For studies of the hippie and drug cultures, see Nicholas von Hoffman, *We Are the People Our Parents Warned Us Against* (New York: Crest, 1969) and Tom Wolfe, *The Electric Kool-Aid Acid Test* (New York: Bantam, 1969); of the communal culture, see Pitts, "The Counter Culture," and Rosabeth Kantor, *Commitment and Community* (Cambridge: Harvard University Press, 1972). On the political culture, see Kenneth Kenniston, *The Young Radicals* (New York: Harcourt, Brace and World, 1968). A useful anthology on the musical innovations of these cultures is R. Serge Denisoff and Richard Peterson, eds., *The Sounds of Change* (Chicago: Rand McNally, 1972). Among more general books about the new cultures are Philip Slater, *The Pursuit of Loneliness* (Boston: Beacon Press, 1970), Theodore Roszak, *The Making of a Counter Culture* (New York: Doubleday, 1969), and Charles Reich, *The Greening of America* (New York: Random House, 1971). The latter became a best-seller, perhaps because its conception and advocacy of the new cultures was strongly influenced by the author's participation in various partial cultures. The Consciousness III he advocates is not exactly a partial culture, however, but it is less total than Roszak's counterculture. Since the publication of Roszak's book, counter-

culture has become a synonym for youth culture, although Roszak's definition is much more specific.

19. As Nathan Glazer has pointed out, Reich's *Greening of America* is actually an example of upper-middle culture which expresses the same hostility and snobbery toward lower-middle and low culture as the upper-middle public of mainstream society. See Nathan Glazer, "The Peanut Butter Statement," in Philip Nobile, ed., *The Con III Controversy* (New York: Pocket Books, 1971), pp. 129-136.

20. Much of the literature on both sides is vituperative, but for a thoughtful analysis of the radical position, see Richard Flacks, "Social and Cultural Meanings of Student Revolt," *Social Problems* 17 (Winter 1970): 340-357. An excellent discussion of the critics' point of view is Norman Birnbaum, "Is There a Post-Industrial Revolution?" *Social Policy* 1 (July-August 1970): 11-12.

21. Charles Keil, *Urban Blues* (Chicago: University of Chicago Press, 1966) and Charlie Gillett, *The Sound of the City* (New York: Outerbridge and Dienstfrey, 1970).

22. Bradley S. Greenberg and Brenda Dervin, *Use of the Mass Media by the Urban Poor* (New York: Praeger, 1970). On the role of the media in changing black identity, see Benjamin Singer, "Mass Society, Mass Media and the Transformation of Minority Identity," *British Journal of Sociology* 24 (June 1973): 140-150.

23. Herbert J. Gans, *The Uses of Television and Their Educational Implications* (New York: Center for Urban Education, 1968), p. 32 and appendix c.

24. See, for example, Andrew Greeley, *Why Can't They Be Like Us?* (New York: Dutton, 1971).

25. See, for example, Joseph Lopreato, *Italian-Americans* (New York: Random House, 1970); Dennis Wrong, "How Important Is Social Class?" *Dissent* 19 (Winter 1972): 278-285; and Irving Levine and Judith Herman, "The Life of White Ethnics, *Dissent* 19 (Winter 1972): 286-294.

26. For example, in the summer of 1972, Ezra Pound, the poet whose politics were once openly fascist and anti-Semitic, was refused a prestigious prize awarded by one of the academies that exist in high culture. This refusal occasioned much debate among high culture critics, some supporting it, others arguing either that Pound's poetry deserved the prize even if his politics did not, or that poetry and poets should not be judged by political values.

27. Herbert J. Gans, "How Well Does Television Cover the News?" *New York Times Magazine* 119 (January 11, 1970): 30-45.

28. See, for example, Clayton Riley, "Shaft Can Do Everything: I Can Do Nothing," *New York Times* 121 (August 13, 1972), section 2: 9.

29. Nancy Mitford, *Noblesse Oblige* (New York: Harper & Brothers, 1956). For a recent example, see Daniel Maneker, "Next Week, of Course, It May Be Out To Be In," *New York Times* 123 (January 13, 1974), section 2: 17.

30. Sontag, "'Camp,'" p. 516. I am indebted to David Riesman for calling my attention to this quotation.

31. Wanderer, "In Defense of Popular Taste."

32. However, when critics review the offerings of a higher taste culture not shared by their readers, they are often negative and use their reviews to demonstrate the faults of the higher culture.

33. The audience's evaluation of popular culture content has been studied tangentially by sociologists interested in the flow of influence. See Elihu Katz and Paul Lazarsfeld, *Personal Influence* (Glencoe, Ill.: The Free Press, 1955).

34. For an interesting statement of the credo of the popular culture creator and his or her relationship to the audience and the high culture critic, see the interviews with Morris Lapidus and Alan Lapidus, in John W. Cook and Heinrich Klotz, *Conversations with Architects* (New York: Praeger, 1973), pp. 147-177. Morris Lapidus is and views himself as a designer of popular architecture, primarily for lower-middle and low taste publics. An interview with Robert Venturi and Denise Scott Brown, in Cook and Klotz, *Conversations with Architects*, pp. 247-266, describes two high culture architects who translate lower-middle and low culture architectural styles into high culture forms.

35. Clement Greenberg has described this similarity, and by implication also refers to what I called creator- and user-oreintations in aesthetics, although the latter he calls "kitsch" or synthetic art. Thus, he writes:

> Ultimately, it can be said that the cultivated spectator derives the same values from Picasso that the peasant gets from Repin, since what the latter enjoys in Repin is somehow art too, on however low a scale, and he is sent to look at pictures by the same instincts that send the cultivated spectator. But the ultimate values which the cultivated spectator derives . . . are not immediately or externally present in Picasso's painting, but must be projected into it by the spectator sensitive enough to react sufficiently to plastic qualities . . . . In Repin, on the other hand, the "reflected" effect has already been included in the picture, ready for the spectator's unreflective enjoyment. Where Picasso paints cause, Repin paints effect. Repin predigests art for the spectator and spares him effort, provides him with a short cut to the pleasure of art that detours what is necessarily difficult in genuine art. Repin, or kitsch, is synthetic art.

Clement Greenberg, "Avant-Garde and Kitsch," in Rosenberg and White, *Mass Culture*, pp. 98-107, quote on p. 105.

CHAPTER THREE
The Evaluation of Taste Cultures and Publics

1. I do not claim that the evaluation proceeds from the analytic scheme, for the two are interrelated. Although I have refrained from explicit value judgments in the sociological analysis of taste cultures, implicit ones run through it, and the analysis itself is strongly influenced by my views about high and popular culture.

2. In making this judgment, I do not agree, however, with Van den Haag and other critics who argue that the gratifications of popular culture are spurious. I

believe that all cultures provide genuine gratifications, and I am only suggesting that the higher cultures may do so more effectively.

3. In the same vein, David Riesman has argued that colleges should be judged in terms of the "value added" they provide to or for their students, and that the personal autonomy of an individual should be defined as incremental to a person's own situation and what can be expected of him, rather than by absolute standards. See, for example, David Riesman, with Nathan Glazer, *Faces in the Crowd* (New Haven: Yale University Press, 1952), chapter 6.

4. If only the content of the reward is measured, and the person's background and experience is left out, it is possible that individuals from a high culture public derive more reward from their content choice than do persons from a lower culture public. The difference stems, however, not from the content but from the training the former have received in the aesthetic standards of their culture. As a result, they draw more from culture and are able to relate what they have drawn to many other facets of their emotional and intellectual lives. This extra benefit derives not from their being members of the high culture public, however, but from their training in aesthetics. If the members of other taste publics were given the same amount and quality of aesthetic training cued to their own standards, and if they had the benefit of the scholarship and criticism in their taste culture that is available in high culture, they would benefit in the same way as the former.

5. The conservatives want public policy to maximize the resources, freedom, and power of high culture creators but do not mention social and economic policies that would increase the size of the high culture public. In other words, they want society to support high culture without permitting universal participation in it, a position that bears some resemblance to taxation without representation.

6. The term *relationism* is borrowed from Karl Mannheim, *Ideology and Utopia* (New York: Harcourt, Brace, 1936), pp. 70-71.

7. See here Wilensky's finding that in Detroit college-educated people do not choose high culture material. Harold Wilensky, "Mass Society and Mass Culture," *American Sociological Review* 29 (April 1964): 191.

8. See Herbert J. Gans, *More Equality* (New York: Pantheon, 1973).

9. Interestingly enough, here one of the major critics of popular culture agrees. He writes, "One can live happily and well without high culture. Socrates' plea that the unexamined life is not worth living after all came from a professional examiner of life, an intellectual and perhaps platonic lover of it, a man with an axe to grind. For him, perhaps, the unexamined life was not worth living. For most people it is." Van den Haag, in Rosenberg and White, *Mass Culture*, p. 528. Van den Haag's identification of self-examination with high culture is gratuitous, however, and reflects his own feelings about people who do not share high culture. There is self-examination outside high culture as well.

10. For a fuller statement of this argument, see Herbert J. Gans, *People and Plans* (New York: Basic Books, 1968), chapter 9.

11. M. Jahoda, P. Lazarsfeld, and H. Zeisel, *Marienthal: The Sociography of an Unemployed Community* (Chicago: Aldine-Atherton, 1971).

12. Programming is also a term used in computer language, but I do not use it in this sense here, and do not want to imply that culture can be programmed on a computer.

13. For a somewhat similar proposal, see Stuart Hall and Paddy Whannel, *The Popular Arts* (New York: Pantheon Books, 1965), chapters 2 and 3.

14. See, for example, Louis Harris, "But Do We Like What We Watch?" *Life* 71 (September 11, 1971): 40-44 and Robert T. Bower, *Television and the Public* (New York: Holt, Rinehart and Winston, 1973).

15. For more detailed analysis of the rating system and its use in television programming, see Martin Mayer, *About Television* (New York: Harper & Row, 1972), chapter 2 and Les Brown, *Television* (New York: Harcourt, Brace Jovanovich, 1971).

16. Herbert J. Gans, *The Uses of Television and Their Educational Implications* (New York: Center for Urban Education, 1968), pp. 40-49.

17. Here I draw on George Gerbner's research proposals for cultural indicators. See, for example, George Gerbner, "Toward 'Cultural Indicators,'" in George Gerbner, et al., eds., *The Analysis of Communication Content* (New York: John Wiley and Sons, 1969), pp. 123-132.

18. Eric Larrabee, "Journalism: Toward the Definition of a Profession," *Studies in Public Communication* no. 3 (Summer 1961): 23-26. Although the title does not indicate it, this article is a thoughtful analysis of the feedback problem as viewed by the professional writer.

Index

Adorno, Theodore, 54, 162
Advertising, media, 35-36, 139, 152,
153
Aesthetic, defined, 14
Aesthetic relationism, 129, 132
Aesthetic standards: differences among,
67-69; and education, 128-129; and
high culture, 78-79, 117-118; and
low culture, 90, 118; lower-middle
culture, 84-85; and mass culture
critique, 51-52, 61-62; sharing of,
111; and social class, 70-71
Agenda setting, by mass media, 37
Agnew, Spiro, 89
"All in the Family," 88, 106, 135
Arendt, Hannah, 162
Art, 21, 31, 42, 45, 53, 81, 82, 87-88,
150
Atlantic, 84
Audience research, 147-149, 151

Baker, Robert, 164
Baldwin, James, 80
Ball, Sandra J., 164
Bauer, Alice H., and Raymond A., 162,
165
Becker, Howard S., 163
Bell, Daniel, 5-6, 161, 164, 167
Berelson, Bernard, 165
Bergman, Ingmar, 83, 115
Berkeley, Busby, 109
Birnbaum, Norman, 169
Black culture, 94, 100-101, 104, 152,
155-156, 159; films, 108; music, 100

Blacks, 8, 94, 104-108, 133-135
Bluestone, George, 168
Bogart, Humphrey, 109
Bogart, Leo, 164
"Bonanza," 87
Borrowing, cultural, 27-28, 83, 110,
115
Bower, Robert T., 172
British Broadcasting Corporation, 136
Brooks, Van Wyck, 167
Brown, Denise Scott, 170
Brown, Les, 172
Bryson, Lyman, 166
Bureaucratization, of society, 99

Cantor, Muriel, 163
Carnal Knowledge, 113
Cawelti, John G., 161
Censorship, 105, 112-113, 139, 144
Chace, William M., 165
Chaffee, Steven, 37, 165
Chaplin, Charlie, 110
Civil liberties, 144-145
Clark, Kenneth, 163
Class, defined, 167
Cleaver, Eldridge, 107
Cohen, Bernard, 165
Commercial enterprise, 47, 97, 111;
high culture as, 21-22, 29-30, 80-81
Communes, 95, 96, 98
Community Antenna Television (CATV),
157
Content analysis, of cultural products,
147

Cooper, Gary, 91
Corporation for Public Broadcasting, 155
Cosmopolitan, 86, 88
Counterculture, 97, 98
Cousins, Norman, 168
Craig, David, 165
Creators: creator- versus user-orientation, 20-21, 25-27, 28-30, 62-64, 73, 75-76, 78-79, 80-81, 96-97, 109-110, 122-123, 135, 140-141, 147-148; defined, 14; in high versus popular cultures, 23-27, 28-30; as poorly served, 150-151; writer-producer conflict, 24-25
Critics, role of, 27-28, 78, 83-84, 116-118, 151
Cultural borrowing, 27-28, 115
Cultural change, 76-77, 80-81
Cultural conflict, 3-4; and democracy, 144; and economic conflict, 113; pornography regulation, 112-113; and taste publics, 112
Cultural diversity, 22-23, 67-68, 140
Cultural equality, 8-9, 34, 114-115, 129-130, 141, 142
Cultural evaluation, 121-122, 128-129
Cultural mobility, 114-115; defined, 129-130; and leisure, 130-132; trends in, 130-132
Cultural planning: and cultural innovation, 148-149; research for, 146-149
Cultural pluralism, 9, 13, 42, 69, 132-135, 156-159
Cultural policy: aesthetic training, 127; creator- versus user-interests, 122-123; criteria for, 122-124; cultural evaluation, 121-122; cultural vitality, 123; education, and cultural choice, 126-127; and high culture, 121-124; and mass culture critique, 121-124; and public interest, 123; and revolution, 130-131; taste levels, 124; value judgments concerning, 125-129
Cultural reform, 131, 136-137
Cultural straddling, 81, 109
Cultural vitality, 28-29, 63-64, 123, 140

Culture: American, 8, 9, 13, 46, 59, 71, 114; black, 94, 100-101, 104, 152, 155-156, 159; communal, 95, 96; drug, 94-98; escapist, 137; ethnic, 101-103, 134-135; hippie, 93, 94; Jewish, 101, 102; middle class, 42; neo-dadaist, 94-95; official, 45, 113-114, 136; partial versus total, 13, 94-96; political, 95, 96; Puerto Rican, 94, 100, 134; religious, 96; and taste culture, 12-15

Democracy, 44, 48, 50-51, 100, 143, 144, 145
Denisoff, R. Serge, 166, 168
Denney, Reuel, 162, 163, 165, 167
Dervin, Brenda, 163, 169
Diversity, cultural, 22-23, 67-68, 140
Drug culture, 94, 95, 96, 97, 98
Duncan, Hugh Dalziel, 162, 163, 166, 167
Dylan, Bob, 97

Education, and cultural choice, 126-127
Eliot, T. S., 29, 54, 70, 162
Elitism, 52-55, 59-60, 61-62
Ellul, Jacques, 44, 49-51, 54, 165
Equality, cultural, 34, 114-115, 141, 142; and cultural mobility policy, 129-130; and high culture, 8-9; and the poor, 130; in taste cultures, 127-128
Ethnic cultures, 101-103

Fantasy, 35
Faulkner, Robert, 163
Federal Communications Commission (FCC), 48, 111, 113
Feedback, 32, 138-139, 147-148, 151
Feininger, Lyonel, 87
Feldman, Jacob, 165
Ferdinand, Theodore N., 164
Feshbach, Seymour, 164
Fiedler, Leslie, 162
Films, 78, 86-89, 90, 91, 92-93, 108; and personal freedom, 58-60

Fiske, Marjorie, 4, 161
Flacks, Richard, 169
Folk culture, 11, 25, 27-28, 31, 42, 45, 52-53, 55-56, 60, 75, 83, 94, 102, 135
Freidson, Eliot, 35, 164

Gable, Clark, 91
Gaudet, Hazel, 165
Gerbner, George, 172
Gillett, Charlie, 169
Glazer, Nathan, 5, 6, 161, 162, 163, 165, 167, 169, 171
Goldhamer, Herbert, 163
Government, and culture, 45-51, 136, 153-156; and television, 47-48
Graffiti, 93
Greeley, Andrew, 169
Greenberg, Bradley S., 163, 169
Greenberg, Clement, 54, 162, 170

Hair, 83
Hall, Stuart, 172
Hammett, Dashiel, 81
Handlin, Oscar, 162
Hare Krishna cult, 96
"Harlem on My Mind," 85
Harper's, 84, 110
Harris, Louis, 168, 172
Hayden, Tom, 168
Hemingway, Ernest, 80
Herman, Judith, 169
Herzog, Herta, 164
Hesse, Hermann, 84
High culture: aesthetic standards, 117-118; audience for, 21-23; avant-garde, 81, 94, 124; borrowing, 27-28; camp, 80; changes in, 76-77, 80-81; and class, 52-55, 60, 129, 136; classics, 22-23; as commercial enterprise, 21-22, 29-30, 80-81; compared to popular culture, 6, 9, 10, 20-23, 25, 27-28, 42-43, 52-55, 60, 62-64, 67-69, 109-110; creator- versus user-orientation, 25-27, 62-64, 75-76, 78-79, 80-81, 140-141; critic's role, 78, 116-118; and cultural policy, 121-122, 123,

124; distribution of, 77-78, 80-81; and equality, 8-9; escapist culture, 137; films, 78; folk culture, 27-28, 42, 55-56, 60; function of, 125-126; and the humanities, 74; influence of, 8-9, 115-118; as low-wage industry, 29-30; and mental illness, 39-40; music, 81; political values, 105, 106; and the poor, 69; social issues, 145-146; and the social sciences, 74, 77; standardization in, 22-23; straddling, 81, 109; as taste culture, 75-81; and television, 78, 135; vitality of, 28-29, 63-64
Himmelweit, Hilde, 164
Hippies, 93, 94, 97
Hirsch, Paul M., 163
Hitler, Adolf, 46
Hoffman, Nicholas von, 168
Hollingshead, August B., 163, 167
Hope, Bob, 112
Horkheimer, Max, 54
Howe, Irving, 54, 162
Hyman, Stanley Edgar, 162

Innovation, cultural, 148-149, 150-151, 155-156; in high versus popular cultures, 22-23

Jacobs, Norman, 162, 166
Jahoda, Marie, 171
Jarrell, Randall, 162
Jewish culture, 101, 102
Joplin, Janis, 97
Jouvenal, Bertrand de, 161
Joyce, James, 22

Kantor, Rosabeth, 168
Katz, Elihu, 164, 165, 170
Keil, Charles, 169
Kenniston, Kenneth, 168
Kesey, Ken, 168
Kirk, Russell, 54
Klapper, Joseph, 162, 164, 165
Kornhauser, William, 165
Kramer, Hilton, 167

Lang, Gladys Engel, and Kurt, 165
Langner, Thomas S., 163
Lapidus, Alan, and Morris, 170
Larrabee, Eric, 148, 172
Lawrence, D. H., 22
Lazarsfeld, Paul, 162, 164, 165, 170
Leavis, R. F., 54, 162
Leisure, 4, 130-132
Leites, Nathan, 166
Lerner, Daniel, 57, 166
Lester, Marilyn, 165
Levine, Irving, 169
Levine, Mark, 166
Liebow, Elliot, 163
Life, 86, 89
Lindsay, John, 103
Look, 86
Lopreato, Joseph, 169
Low culture, 71, 149-150; action
    drama, 90-91; aesthetic standards,
    90, 118; film, television, and art,
    90, 91, 92-93; and mass media, 91-
    92; political values, 104; porno-
    graphy, 112-113; sexual segregation,
    90, 92-93; as taste public, 89; word-
    of-mouth criticism, 116-117
Lowenthal, Leo, 4, 20, 54, 161, 162
Lower-middle culture, 71; aesthetic
    standards, 84-85; form and sub-
    stance, 85-86; and mass media, 86;
    and museums, 85; reading, film,
    television, and art, 86-89; sex, 86,
    88
Lunt, Paul S., 166
Lyle, Jack, 164
Lynes, Russell, 167

McCarthy, Joseph, 7, 46
McCombs, Maxwell, 165
MacDonald, Dwight, 10, 20, 30, 54,
    83, 161, 162, 163
McLuhan, Marshall, 40-41, 162
McPhee, William, 165
Madden, David, 161
Mailer, Norman, 80, 83
Maneker, Daniel, 169
Mannheim, Karl, 45, 171
Marcuse, Herbert, 5, 44, 48-49, 107,
    165

Marris, Peter, 165
"Mary Tyler Moore Show," 88
M.A.S.H., 85
Mass culture, 20; defined, 9-10
Mass culture critique, 3-4, 136; aesthe-
    tic standards, 51-52, 61-62; biases
    of, 51-52; creator-orientation, 25-
    26; cultural evolution, 128-129;
    cultural policy, 121-122, 123-124;
    elitism in, 52-55, 59-60, 61-62; and
    equality, 8-9; European versus
    American, 54-55; future of, 4-9;
    historical fallacy of, 55-60; and in-
    tellectuals, 7-8; major themes of,
    19; Marcuse and Ellul on, 48-51;
    political bias, 55, 104; taste levels,
    61-62; youth culture, 5, 6, 7
Mass media: advertising, 35-36, 139;
    blacks, 105-106; censorship, 105,
    139; children, effects on, 33, 35,
    40; cohesive function, 142; as com-
    mercial enterprise, 47, 111; and
    crime, 32-34; decentralization of,
    151; democracy, 144, 145; eco-
    nomic power of, 113; effects of,
    30-45, 139-140, 143; fantasy, 35;
    feedback, 32, 138-139; govern-
    ment's role, 45-51; influence of
    high culture, 115-118; innovation
    in, 150-151; and low culture, 91-
    92; and lower-middle culture, 86;
    middle class culture, 42; as non-
    profit institution, 48, 152; political
    pressures, 105-106; and the poor,
    31-32, 34, 39, 40, 58, 107, 134;
    role models, 57-59; and sexual be-
    havior, 34-35; and social trends, 46,
    47; subcultural programming, 138,
    151, 152-153; and taste cultures,
    11-12; television violence and ag-
    gressive behavior, 32-34
Mass society, 9-10, 31-32, 43-45, 57
"Maude," 88
Mayer, Martin, 172
Meehan, Thomas, 167
Mental illness, 31, 33, 39-40
Meritocracy, credentialism versus per-
    formance, 9
Merton, Robert K., 165
Meyersohn, Rolf, 162, 164

Michael, Stanley T., 163
Middle America, 8, 9, 46, 59, 114
Miller, Arthur, 83
Mitford, Nancy, 109, 169
Molotch, Harvey, 165
Morris, Willie, 167
Ms., 84
Music, 81, 82-83, 97, 98, 123, 150

National Endowment for the Humanities, 154
News media, 142; agenda setting, 37; function of, 39; journalist's personal values, 37-39; political advertising, 36-37; political values, 106-107; and the poor, 39
Newsweek, 82
New York, 84
New York Daily News, 116
New York Review of Books, 80
New York Times, 83, 143
New Yorker, 84
Nielsen ratings, television, 138

Official culture, 45, 113-114, 136
Oldenburg, Klaes, 28
Oppenheim, A., 164
Ortega y Gasset, Jose, 45, 54, 162, 165

Parker, Edwin, 164
Peterson, Richard, 168
Pitts, Jesse, 168
Playboy, 84, 92
Pluralism, cultural, 9, 13, 42, 69, 132-135, 156-159
Political advertising, television, 36-37
Political culture, 95-96
Politics, 12-13, 55, 103-108, 111-112, 154-157
Pool, Ithiel De Sola, 162
Popular culture: audience for, 21-23; borrowing, 27-28; classics, 22-23; as commercial enterprise, 20-21; creator- versus user-orientation, 20-21, 26-27, 62-64; defined, 9, 10, 14; and democracy, 44, 48, 50-51; effects of, 30-36; versus high cul-

ture, 6, 9, 10, 20-23, 25, 27-28, 42-43, 52-55, 60, 62-64, 67-69, 109-110; and mental illness, 31, 33, 39-40; modernization, 55-60; and propaganda, 50-51; and revolution, 49, 107-108; standardization in, 22-23; straddling, 109; taste levels, 44-45; and technology, 44; and totalitarianism, 45-48
Pornography, 34-35, 112-113
Pound, Ezra, 169
Poverty, 31-32, 34, 39, 40, 58, 69, 107, 113, 130, 132, 134, 149-150, 152, 154, 155, 157, 159
Presley, Elvis, 6
Procaccino, Mario, 103
Propaganda, 36, 44, 50-51
Psychology Today, 82
Public service programming, television, 111, 113
Public television, 48, 152, 153, 157
Puerto Rican culture, 94, 100, 134

Quasi-folk low culture, 71, 93-94, 102, 149-150

Radicalism, 98-100, 104
Rainwater, Lee, 163
Reader's Digest, 86, 110
Redlich, Frederick C., 163, 167
Reich, Charles, 168, 169
Religious culture, 96
Report of the Commission on Obscenity and Pornography, 34, 164
Report of the Surgeon General's Advisory Committee, 1972, 33
Revolution, 49, 107-108, 130-131
Riesman, David, 72, 162-165, 167, 169, 171
Riesman, Evelyn T., 164
Riley, Clayton, 169
Riley, John W., and Matilda, 164
Robbins, Harold, 86, 87, 88
Rockwell, Norman, 85
Rolling Stone, 97
Rosenberg, Bernard, 44, 54, 162, 165
Rosenberg, Harold, 54-55
Roszak, Theodore, 97, 98, 168
Rubin, Jerry, 168

Salinger, J. D., 80
Saturday Evening Post, 86, 89
Schramm, Wilbur, 164
Selective perception, 32, 143, 144
Selznick, Gertrude, and Philip, 166
Sex, 34-35, 86, 88, 90, 92-93, 105
Shaw, Donald, 165
Shils, Edward, 57, 61, 162, 166, 167
Shulman, Irwin, 162
Sinclair, Upton, 145
Singer, Benjamin, 169
Singer, Robert D., 164
Slater, Philip, 168
Soap opera, 58-59
Social cohesion, and the media, 142
Social issues, 107; and high culture, 145-146; and mass media, 46, 47
Social sciences, and high culture, 74, 77
Socialism, and mass culture critique, 54-55
Sociology, taste cultures in, 73-74
Sontag, Susan, 80, 109, 110, 167
Soviet Union, official culture, 136
Spengler, Oswald, 45
Spillane, Mickey, 81
Stalin, Joseph V., 46
Status hierarchy, 114, 115, 117
Stevenson, Adlai, 13
Straddling, cultural, 81, 109
Studs Lonigan, 113
Subcultural programming: and advertising, 139, 152; audience research, 147-149, 151; and blacks, 134-135; censorship, 144; creator- versus user-orientation, 135, 140-141; critic's role, 151; cultural planning, 146-149; cultural reform, 136-137; defined, 132-133; and democracy, 143, 144; equality, 141, 142; ethnic minorities, 134-135; feedback, 151; financing of, 152-156; governmental role, 136, 153-156; and harmful content, 139-140; high culture public, 135; implementation of, 146-149; innovation, 155-156; and mass media, 138, 151, 152-153; news programs, 142; and politics, 154-157; and the poor, 134, 152; for poorly served taste publics, 149-152; profitability of, 151-152; pros-

pects for, 156-159; and social cohesion, 142; taste cultures and publics, 133-135; taste hierarchy, 141-142; and technology, 158; and television, 133, 157
Sullivan, Ed, 112
Susann, Jacqueline, 86, 87, 88

Taste culture: boundaries, 12-15, 71-72; conservative versus radical, 104; content changes, 72-73; creator- versus user-orientation, 73, 109-110; defined, 68-69, 70-75; desirability criteria, 122-124; education, 70-71; equality, 127-128; function, 67-69; high culture, 75-81; identification, 146-147; low culture, 71; lower-middle culture, 71; and mass media, 11-12; numbers of, 69, 71; political values, 12-13; politics, 103-108; quasi-folk low culture, 71; social class, 70-71; social problems, 145-146; as subculture, 13; taste hierarchy, 70-71; versus taste publics, 69-75; upper-middle culture, 71, 81; vicarious, 14; and youth culture, 70, 71
Taste hierarchy, 70-71, 141-142; class hierarchy, 114; cultural inequality, 114-115; influence of high culture, 115-118; status hierarchy, 115, 117
Taste levels, 44-45, 124, 130-131, 140-141
Taste publics: defined, 11, 12, 68-69, 70-75, 89; desirability criteria, 122-124; identification of, 146-147; as interest groups, 112; number of, 71; poorly served publics, 149-150
Taste structure: cultural borrowing, 110; cultural straddling, 109; defined, 103, 108; economy, 111-112; hierarchy, 108; mobility of choice, 110; multicultural appeal, 110-111; and social class, 108-109
Television: audience feedback, 138; blacks, 105-106; cassette, 157; CATV, 157; globalization of world, 40-41; and government, 47-48; and high culture, 78, 135; versus politi-